oogy

the only a family could love

LARRY LEVIN

GC

GRAND CENTRAL
PUBLISHING

New York   Boston

Grand Central Publishing
Hachette Book Group
237 Park Avenue
New York, NY 10017

www.HachetteBookGroup.com

Printed in the United States of America

First Edition: October 2010
10 9 8 7 6 5 4 3 2 1

Grand Central Publishing is a division of Hachette Book Group, Inc.
The Grand Central Publishing name and logo is a trademark of Hachette Book Group, Inc.

Library of Congress Cataloging-in-Publication Data

Levin, Larry (Laurence M.)
  Oogy : the dog only a family could love / Larry Levin. — 1st ed.
     p. cm.
  Summary: "A heartwarming story of a puppy brought back from the brink of death, and the family he adopted"— Provided by the publisher.
  ISBN 978-0-446-54631-7
  1. Pit bull terriers—Pennsylvania. 2. Puppies—Pennsylvania. 3. Dog adoption—Pennsylvania. 4. Animal welfare—Pennsylvania. 5. Levin, Larry. 6. Levin, Larry—Family. 7. Human-animal relationships—Pennsylvania. 8. Ardmore Animal Hospital (Ardmore, Pa.) I. Title.
  SF429.P58L48 2010
  636.70092'9—dc22

                                                        2010003721

Book design by Giorgetta Bell McRee

To Jennifer, Noah, and Dan, whose love has kept me alive and whose confidence in me has sustained me. The joy they have taken in their own experiences as well as their delight in and appreciation of our time together has imbued me with a sense of wonder.

To Oogy, of course, who has shared so much devotion, affection, and strength, and has trusted us so unhesitatingly and completely that it became another reward. Our spirits have been commingled, and we are all the better for it.

For all people who strive to comfort and help suffering animals: the lost and the frightened, the abused and the hunted, the abandoned and the captured, and those that should be in a better place than where they are.

CONTENTS

ACKNOWLEDGMENTS

Thanks to:

My family and friends, who always knew I could do this and without whose loving support I couldn't have;

Those encountered along the way who contributed to the marvelous adventures in which I have been lucky enough to participate;

Those who shared their wisdom so that I had at least a fighting chance to understand how and why my life has unfolded as it has;

Dr. James Bianco and Diane Klein and the staff at Ardmore Animal Hospital, who made this possible and were never too busy to answer my questions;

Kent Wolf, my agent, who believed in this story even when he had no idea if I could tell it; and,

Emily Griffin, my editor, who challenged me and taught me and helped me say what I wanted to say and, in so doing, made me a better writer.

This book would not have been possible without any of you.

CHAPTER 1 *Morning*

Whorizonten the alarm goes off at 5:30 a.m., it is still dark outside. Lying there, I take a quick mental inventory of what lies before me this morning. The boys don't have to be at school early for a team meeting or to see any of their teachers. They don't have to finish any homework or cram last minute for a test. As seniors in high school and already admitted to college, they are coasting to the finish line. In a way, they have already passed it. The breakfast table to raise money for the lacrosse team does not start until tomorrow, to coincide with the opening game of the season. So with both my morning and afternoon committed tomorrow, I have lots to get done today. But it also means that, right now, I have the luxury of hitting the snooze button for another ten minutes' sleep.

The alarm seems to go off again in about fifteen seconds. I force myself to sit up. It feels as if I'm underwater, struggling to surface. I wriggle my toes and fingers, which I once read helps to keep you awake; I run my hands over my face and rub the sleep from my eyes. I nudge Jennifer, who without turning over asks for another fifteen minutes of sleep. Groggily, I push aside the comforter on my side; I swing my legs over the edge of the bed and drop to the floor. Stumbling around and over barely visible mounds of towels, sweats, T-shirts, socks, and athletic wear, I pass through the laundry room into the bathroom. There, I turn on the light, brush my teeth, and throw cold water on my face. Back in the laundry room, I pull off the T-shirt I slept in and put on a clean one from among the piles of clothing stacked up everywhere — on the built-in bench, atop the radiator cover, along both windowsills, and in front of the radiator. After a bit of a search, I pull out a pair of clean socks and sweatpants and lean against the dryer to pull them on.

I walk out of the bedroom, leaving the door halfway open behind me. From the landing on the second floor, I can see that the downstairs light is on. There are four couches on our first floor. On rare occasions, Noah and Dan will sleep on the same couch down there; sometimes they sleep in different rooms; but usually they're both sacked out in the family room, one on the old couch, the other on the futon sofa bed, alternating each night. There's no way to predict which one of the boys Oogy will have chosen to sleep with, but he'll be next to one of them.

At the foot of the stairs, I first glance to my right into what used to be the living room. The doors are wide open, and no one is sleeping there. The lights in the family room, to my left, are controlled by toggle switches on the wall in the hallway; I turn up the rear bank of lights ever so slightly and peer inside. I think I see Noah stretched out on the futon opened up on the floor, wrapped in two blankets, which would mean that Dan is on the old couch adjacent to the rear glass wall. Behind Dan on the couch, stretched lengthwise, one paw draped over Dan's shoulders, Oogy is barely distinguishable from the white comforter covering Dan. No one so much as stirs. I toggle the lights back down and click them off.

In the kitchen I put cold water into the coffeemaker, measure out coffee into the filter, and press the "on" button. The amber light comes on, the water roils, and the aroma of brewing coffee begins to waft through the air reassuringly. I turn on the radio to get a weather update that I can pass on to the boys. This radio must be at least forty years old; it used to sit in the kitchen of the home I grew up in, and I have no idea how I have it still. The reception is poor, scratchy and thin, as though the voices inside are being played from an old phonograph record.

I return to the family room and turn on both the front and rear sets of lights halfway. This time, Oogy lifts his head and looks at me. He is still somewhat distant with sleep, but welcome shines in his eyes like candles. His tail thumps softly against the back of the couch. Smiling, I walk over to him and sit on the arm of the sofa, trace my fingers against the thickness of his neck. I touch the well of power just behind there, high on his back between his shoulders. His strength never ceases to amaze me. It seems almost incompatible with his gentle nature.

"Hello, doggy boy," I murmur. "You're a lucky dog, you're a good doggy. You're a good boy. A good boy. Thank you for protecting the boys last night. I'm glad I don't have to worry about that anymore." I bend over him and touch my nose to a spot just behind his neck. He makes that grunting sound that signifies absolute contentment; when I lift my face from between his shoulders, he raises his head and licks my nose. In return, I nuzzle the side of his face that still has an ear.

"I've got to get everyone going," I tell him. "You and I will go out later, okay?"

He cocks his head, the ear standing up at alert. I cup it with one hand and knead it gently. I have been told that there are many nerve endings in a dog's ears and that by rubbing them, one can relax the whole dog. Because Oogy has only one ear, the task is simplified, but at the same time it raises some odd questions. Can only half of Oogy get relaxed by rubbing his remaining ear? If so, would that be his right side, the side that still has an ear? Or are dogs left-eared and right-eared the way humans are left- and right-brained, so that his right ear controls the left side of his body? Clearly, there are many things about dogs that I have yet to learn.

"Don't get excited just yet," I caution him. "There are things that I need to get done before we can party." When I rise he does, too, stretching with a soft grunt. Then he reverses himself and curls up with his head next to Dan's hip. He sighs contentedly before he closes his eyes and drifts off to sleep again.

Neither boy has moved. "Yo," I say to them. "Time for breakfast. Who's having what?"

There is no response.

"Breakfast time," I repeat, a little louder. From the incoherent mumbling that rises briefly in response, I determine that the boys have lived through the night, although it is still impossible to tell whether they may have entered into permanent vegetative states.

"Breakfast orders, please," I repeat, louder still.

"Don't yell!" Noah moans without lifting his head from the pillow or even turning it in my direction.

"I'm not yelling," I explain. "*This would be yelling!*" Oogy's head jerks up, trying to understand whether he should be concerned about the change in timbre. I drop my voice back to normal. "I'm just trying to get your attention." Oogy's head goes back on the pillow, reacting to the sound of my voice as though controlled by a string. His ear flops over against the side of his head.

I manage to get the boys' breakfast requests, then turn on the TV for them as I head out the door. Back in the kitchen, I glance out the window. The light is dim, the sky overcast and cloudy, as though freighted with rain. I put water into a pot, add some milk and a little salt, and then drop in a few raisins to fatten in the water as it boils. After securing the lid and striking a match, I ignite the gas burner; the blue flame pops up. I wrap four strips of bacon in a paper towel and place them on a plate in the microwave, then set the timer for three minutes and thirty seconds. Every brand of bacon has a different cook time for the same number of strips. Then there's the variable of how long the bacon has been in the refrigerator since the package was opened—that too must be factored in. The fresher the bacon, the longer it takes to cook. What does it say about me that I have learned over the years that there is a kind of personality to bacon?

The pulsing of the water in the coffeemaker is accompanied by a sighing sound from inside it, as though, resignedly, it is finishing its assigned task. I hear the volume of the TV rise and make a quick foray back to the family room. Both boys are sitting up on the old couch now, facing the TV; a sports talk show is on. They are, to be generous about it, half-awake, each wrapped in a comforter, looking like refugees. Behind them, his head directly above and between where their shoulders touch, Oogy sits alert, watching me. Illuminated by the murky light behind them, the outlines of Oogy and the boys blur together; they look like one being, a three-headed mutant.

On the way out of the room, I push the light switch toggles all the way on in hopes that it will help the boys to wake up. I walk to the foot of the stairs and yell up to Jennifer, who reluctantly confirms that she is, in fact, awake. Her voice sounds muffled, as though she's under a blanket. I return to the kitchen, where I am once again buoyed by the smell of the coffee. I pull Oogy's food bowl from the drainer in the sink and prepare his breakfast, after which I place it on the floor by the water dish. By now, the water in the pot is boiling. I add some cinnamon and rolled oats to the pot, stirring the contents until the mixture starts to thicken, then I turn down the flame. I hit the button on the microwave to start the bacon cooking, open the toaster oven and slide two muffins inside. I am the maestro of the breakfast symphony.

I put sugar on the tray for Noah's oatmeal and some maple syrup into a glass for Dan to add to his. I pour Noah a glass of cranberry juice and a glass of nonfat milk; Dan gets some orange juice and a glass of milk as well. Each boy gets a multivitamin and, thanks to their sports injuries, two of the same joint pills I give Oogy for his aching knees.

The coffeemaker emits an electronic death rattle to signify its task is complete just as Jennifer wanders into the kitchen in pajamas and a flannel robe. We exchange morning greetings. She has an 8:30 meeting she has not yet prepared for, so she needs to get going. I assure her that everything is under control. She pours herself a cup of coffee, adds milk from a plastic quart, and heads back upstairs after stopping by the family room to check on the boys. I return the milk to the fridge and pour myself a steaming cup of coffee as well. Then I take a sip, black, unsweetened, feeling it slide down to my feet and shoot back up to my brain; it seems to resound like a hammered weight striking the gong at the top of a "Test Your Strength" game at a cartoon carnival. I am officially awake.

The microwave beeps. Before I pull out the bacon, I stir the oatmeal one last time and turn off the range. I dry the bacon in another set of paper towels and heat the maple syrup in the microwave. After I drop the paper towels in the trash, I add a few dollops of ammonia to the bag to mask the odor and deter Oogy from rooting around inside. Then I hear the soft click of toenails on the tile floor and look up to see Oogy standing by the swinging door to the kitchen. His forelegs look almost comically bowed because of the massive bunched muscles and the enormous square chest from which they stem. His feet appear oversize compared with the rest of his body; he looks as if he is wearing doggy clown shoes. I walk over to him, and he leans his head against my leg. I rub him behind his ear. I rub the little black hole where his left ear used to be, then bend over and, with my nose on his neck, rub the ropelike muscles on either side. Oogy makes "chuffing" sounds like a small steam engine. He is happy.

"You're a good doggy," I tell him. "You're the best doggy." I mean that, and he knows I mean that. "You're in a special place. Aren't you a lucky dog? I know that it's weird to hear that, but you are. Plus," I tell him, "you've got fat feet. Look at those silly feet." Then I say to him, "Let me get everyone out. After that, you and I can hang." He bends to his food bowl, snorting his pleasure, snuffling as he inhales the contents. I return to the morning routine.

By the time I have brought breakfast to the boys and returned to the kitchen, Oogy is standing by the back door. When I walk into the room, he barks once at me to let me know that he wants to go outside, as though I otherwise wouldn't know he is there and would simply overlook eighty-five pounds of white, one-eared dog.

"Okay, okay. Here we go," I tell him. "Let's put the magic collar on." I bend over him and clip the red nylon collar for the electronic fence into place alongside his regular collar, which has a little blue bone-shaped tag with his name and our telephone number on it and a red, heart-shaped rabies vaccination tag. "Be careful out there," I tell him. I tell him the same thing every time he leaves the house to go into the yard, day or night. As parents, Jennifer and I have tried to prepare the boys for what they will encounter in the world once they're on their own, but with Oogy it's different. At least we have had the opportunity to try to teach the boys how to choose; I cannot prepare Oogy to weigh his options and select a safe course, and I do not want anything bad to happen to him ever again. Once he is out the door, I have no control over what he will encounter. As a result, letting him outside often feels like an act of faith.

I pull open the door and Oogy sticks his head out. His nose is in the air, nostrils twitching, reading the news on the wind. His ear is alert, as though somewhere there is a sound he does not fully understand. Then he wriggles past the screen door into the yard. I am still rinsing out his food bowl when the boys, finished with their breakfast, bring in their cereal bowls and glasses, letting them and the spoons clink noisily into the sink.

They are taller than me now. When they were toddlers, most people had a difficult time distinguishing one from the other; the kids in preschool called them by the same name, "DannyNoah," just to be sure they had it right. Both have the same strawberry blond hair that curls when it gets long (Jenny calls it an "Izro," an Israeli Afro). They have the same gray green eyes, the same skin tone. The major distinction between them has always been a barely noticeable variance in height and weight, which is now more pronounced than when they were younger. Noah, who has always been slightly taller than Dan, shot up this past year, adding several inches, and is now noticeably the taller of the two. Jennifer thinks that if Dan had not cut weight for the last four years during wrestling season, he would be as tall as Noah. I think she's right.

They ask me about the weather forecast for the day and head upstairs to dress accordingly. I turn off the radio; I prefer the silence. Blue gray morning light now washes the windows. I rinse off the glasses and dishes the boys have left in the sink and put them in the dishwasher. I amble into the family room to stack pillows behind the old couch, then fold the comforters alongside the pillows. I return the futon bed back into the couch it came from and replace the pillows there. While he was still a puppy, Oogy tore out several chunks from the futon mattress, and every time the boys use it, pieces of yellow foam dot the floor like cake crumbs. I pick these up and dump them in a waste can. As I am doing this, I hear the creak of the back door opening and listen to Oogy walking down the hall.

When he appears in the doorway, I sit on the old couch and pat the open area next to me. "C'mon, puppy dog. Come up."

He comes over to me, those large dark eyes searching for something in my face, and then clambers onto the couch. He leans his right side against the back of the couch, licks his lips several times as though he is savoring something, and, with a sigh, parks his butt on my lap as though he is recharging. I rub his ear, trace a finger over his broad sternum to his silky pink belly, where the spots are more pronounced than those covered by the short white fur on the rest of his body. The left side of his muzzle, the side of his face that has been rebuilt, twitches ever so slightly. I am amazed, as I am every day, at what he has gone through to get here and, despite it, the level of trust he has reposed in us from the start. He turns and gets that goopy look on his face he shows me at such moments, and I pull back just in time to avoid a big, sloppy kiss. I have been told that dogs lick people because they want to know what they taste like, but Oogy has known what we taste like for years and the licking has never diminished. The boys and I are convinced that his licking us is his form of kisses. With a sigh, Oogy momentarily rests his head on the top of the couch. Suddenly, his head jerks up, and he barks at something out there, only he knows what. As is often the case, I have no idea what he is barking at or whether he is just imagining something. But I never fail to thank him for protecting us. After a few more moments of intense listening, he puts his head back down.

The boys clunk downstairs, still not running on all cylinders, and head for the kitchen, where they keep their backpacks. They pull out certain books, insert others, check homework binders, and make sure they have what they need for the day. There is some discussion as to whether it is a "B" or a "C" day, which controls their class schedules. Once they have gotten organized, they come back into the family room for another ten minutes of TV. They know it is time to leave when the highlights portion of the sports show is over. They pull on their sneakers while they watch. Each boy is wearing sweatpants and a T-shirt, but in a different color; this is their unofficial uniform. Jennifer dashes by to gather her laptop and another cup of coffee. She exits the kitchen and races for the driveway with no more than a breathless "Bye!"

In the kitchen, the boys pull on sweatshirts, hitch up their backpacks, and pick up their lacrosse sticks. Dan then suddenly remembers that he has to turn in his wrestling singlets and runs upstairs, where he rifles through the laundry basket until he finds them and then returns to the kitchen. The car they usually drive to school has to go in for inspection today, so they are riding the bus. Oogy climbs off me to be with them in the kitchen, wondering if this will be the day he gets to follow them to wherever it is they go six days a week—five days of school and either practice or a game on Saturday. I follow Oogy into the kitchen. He and I watch as the boys exit the back door to begin the trek up the street to the bus stop.

"Have a good day," I tell them. "See you after practice." Then I ask if either one of them has any requests for dinner. Neither of them does.

"Love you," they each say as they head out the door, and every time I hear that, I am surprised. That they can articulate it. That they direct it at me.

Shortly after the boys have left, and while Oogy and I are still in the kitchen cleaning up, the trash truck stops at the foot of the driveway. In an instant, Oogy has wedged himself through the door and dashed into the yard, barking joyously, the resonance of his barks mingling with the trundling of the can being wheeled up the driveway, the shouts of the workers out in the street, and the grinding of the truck gears. Oogy barks at the man emptying our trash cans as though seeing this is the greatest thing that could ever happen to him. The man talks to Oogy the whole time he is dumping the contents of our several small cans into the one huge canister he wheels along. Oogy says good-bye and comes back into the house.

When he sees me putting on my sneakers, he gets excited, starts dancing and barking, thinking I am going to take him somewhere.

"Calm down," I tell him. "I'm only going out for the paper." He either does not believe me or wants to convince me otherwise, and as soon as we go outside, he starts for the van. "This way, lumpy dog," I call. I head down the driveway toward the front of the house. Oogy runs up alongside me, his tail cutting invisible swaths out of the air, and I stop and rub his forehead; he leans into me, and I gently slap his muscular haunch several times. "You're one strong doggy," I tell him. "I sure am glad you're on our side."

About halfway down the driveway, Oogy stops at the limit dictated by the electronic fence. His eyes follow me attentively as I walk toward the mailbox and pick up the paper off the lawn, and as soon as he sees that I am coming back up the driveway, he walks over to stand under the weeping cherry tree. He does this every morning; he clearly enjoys the way the long, thin tendrils feel against him. He emerges and accompanies me to the back door.

Although he can push open the door with his head when he wants to, and does so routinely, this time he waits for me to open it for him before he scampers inside. He will often do this with the boys as well. I think he takes this action as reassurance that he is safe and taken care of.

As I pour myself another cup of coffee, I look up to see the boys walking back to the house. They must have missed the bus. It is only a small glitch in the day's plan and the type of thing one has to allow for with teenage boys. As they step inside, I gather my ring of keys and wallet without saying a word. Once in the kitchen they apologize, and I tell them it's okay. Oogy is prancing around. The sound of the keys jingling in my hand tells him that we are going for a ride somewhere, and he cannot imagine that he is not going to be included. "You can go," I tell him. He sneezes and wags his head, continues his Oogy four-step. Dan takes off the electronic collar and puts it on the table. Oogy barks once, the sound sharp and hard at the same time, reverberating in the kitchen like a piece of dropped steel.

"What's that, Oogy?" Dan suddenly asks. He drops to one knee in front of Oogy, staring into his face, and cups him under the chin. "You say Timmy's trapped under the hay wagon and the barn is on fire? We'd better get going, then."

Dan rises and goes to the door, and Oogy follows, dashing past him outside. Oogy turns and waits till we catch up, and the four of us walk to the van. The boys go around to the passenger side. I open the rear door on the driver's side for Oogy. He hesitates, afraid of getting a shock. Early on, there were several incidents, for reasons unknown to me, when the current from the electronic fence appeared to have traveled to the collar through the steel of the car frame and hit Oogy like a shovel, even though he was a safe distance away from the fence's perimeter. As a result, he is always somewhat tentative in his approach to any vehicle. And, of course, he does not know that when the collar is off, he cannot get shocked under any circumstances. So I coax him along. He places his front legs inside and waits for me to boost up his rear end. I am not sure if Oogy does this because he knows I will or if it is because climbing into the van puts pressure on his surgically corrected rear joints. Dan, who had called, "Shotgun!" climbs into the passenger's seat; Noah sits behind him. Oogy stands beside me with his forelegs balanced on the front-seat armrests, his rear legs braced on the floor, peering through the windshield for the ten-minute trip. After I drop off the boys, I open the passenger window halfway. Oogy climbs into the vacant seat and, front paws on the door handle, sticks the upper part of his body out of the window, his ear flapping in the wind all the way home.

Once we are back inside the house, Oogy heads for the remainder of last night's bone and I go upstairs to shower. When I am done, I gather up all the used towels I can find from last night and this morning, toss them and some of the boys' sweatpants into the washer, and get a cycle started. I step into the bedroom to get dressed. Oogy is already there, lying on the bed. His eyes follow me. I tell him I need to go to the office and that I feel bad about it, but it cannot be helped. I pull on the clothes I am going to wear for the day and go over to the bed. I touch my nose to Oogy's side and run my hands down his back to the soft skin of his narrow waist. "Time for me to go," I tell him.

As I walk into the hall, he uncoils himself and joins me on the landing, where he waits for me to start down the stairs. As soon as I take the first step, he barrels past me, rushing to the bottom of the steps before following me into the kitchen as though he's attached to me like some white, furry sidecar.

I pour what I promise myself will be my last cup of

coffee, heat it in the microwave, and amble back into the family room. Once I am seated on the couch, Oogy climbs up beside me. This is our morning ritual, a few minutes together, just the two of us. He sits while I lazily trace a finger over his massive chest. His eyes close and open, then close again. Something in the street catches his attention; he stares through the privet hedge outside our house. Then, his curiosity satisfied, he turns around several times and lies down, his head in my lap. I like the way he stretches his massive body. He feels comfortable, relaxed. He feels secure. I am glad that we have been able to do that for him.

With my index finger, I circle where his ear used to be, then run my hands down the muscle of his rib cage and back up to his neck. Lately, he has not been scratching the hole where his left ear was, which is good, because he has a history of infections there. Everything is quiet now. The cartoonlike fervor of morning rush hour has passed. I run through telephone calls I need to make at work, e-mails I must send, letters I should write. I have to mail a form for Noah's lacrosse club; I put my keys over it last night so that I would remember to take it today. Oogy snorts softly several times and lets out a loud sigh. I place my lips just back of his ear hole and breathe into his neck. "Oo-gy pie," I say. "Pie dog. Mr. Pie."

I have heard that when you leave them, dogs do not

know that you are coming back, so every time I leave, I try to let Oogy know that I have every intention of returning. I need to go to work, I explain. I tell him I will be back in the late afternoon to take him for a walk. It will still be light out, I say. The boys will be home while it is still light, too. Mom won't get home until it's dark. I feel compelled to reassure him. I think it is important. Absentmindedly, I trace the scar from the surgery that runs from the top of his skull to underneath his lower jaw.

Oogy is asleep, snoring deeply, and I am reassured by his very presence, moved by the love with which he has repaid us.

Some months after Oogy had come to live with us, Noah looked up at me from where he was lying alongside Oogy and said, "I really feel bad about what happened to Oogy, but if it hadn't happened, he wouldn't be here." The worst thing that ever happened to Oogy was also the best thing. It is but one of the contradictions that have defined his experience. He was a fighting dog who would not fight, with a personality and character that led to the most horrific of experiences imaginable, then saved him.

This is Oogy's story. It is, in the truest sense, a one-in-a-million tale. To tell it accurately necessarily intertwines other stories, those of the people who saved Oogy and all the people who love him, including my family. Part of the wonder has been how, over time, all who have come in contact with Oogy, learned his story, and experienced his genuinely gentle nature and noble bearing have been touched. And because I talk to people every day who have rescued many, many pets of their own, this is a testament to their collective efforts as well.

"You're here now," I tell him. "It's okay."

In his sleep, Oogy's legs begin to twitch; he must be dreaming that he is running. I imagine the scene, because it is so common: It is sunny and late in the day at the dog park; the heat-dried grass scents the wind. Oogy trots across the plateau to where I sit at a picnic table, past a dozen other frolicking dogs, just so that I can touch his head. His distorted face seems to be smiling. Or maybe he really is. I touch my fingers to both sides of his head and kiss him on the nose.

"Go on, you big galoot," I tell him.

Oogy turns to find another dog to play with a while longer.

CHAPTER  *The Patron Saint of Hopeless Causes*

The first time I met Oogy, a veterinarian told me that police had found him in a raid and were directed to take him to Ardmore Animal Hospital (AAH) in Montgomery County, PA, by the local Society for the Prevention of Cruelty to Animals (SPCA). Dr. James Bianco, the surgeon who saved Oogy, told me that he recalled the raid had been on a home because of suspected drug activity. For years, I took the story of Oogy's arrival at Ardmore at face value. It didn't matter to me how Oogy had gotten to the hospital that saved him; it was enough for me that he had been saved. I had no reason to question the explanation with which I had been provided. But eventually, prompted by the curiosity of a reporter friend, I started asking questions to see what I could find out about the chain of events that had culminated in Oogy coming to live with us. I found myself driven to see what I could discover about the actual events themselves. I had to know as much about the truth as I could find out. And even though I learned that it was unlikely the story I'd been told was what had actually happened, I also learned that discovering the actual events surrounding Oogy's arrival might well prove to be impossible.

It would not have been unusual for the police and the SPCA to work in concert during the raid in which Oogy was discovered. Experience had taught the police and the SPCA that wherever dogfighting occurs, there is a substantial chance that other illegal activities are going on, often involving drugs, weapons, and undeclared cash. As a result, the police routinely accompany the SPCA on dogfighting interventions, and the SPCA routinely joins police in, or is available for, drug raids.

Drug dealers fight dogs for money and sometimes simply for bragging rights. They also keep fighting dogs around to protect the drugs and, on occasion, to scare away the competition. This type of operation represents the lowest level of what is now an industry generating over five hundred million dollars a year, commonly referred to as the "street-fighting" aspect of the business. The dogs involved in this lead the most horrific lives imaginable: They are brutalized to toughen them and to make them angry; their injuries are often either not treated or are treated in a rudimentary way (street-fighting dogs have been found with gashes, tears, and cuts stapled together); and they are bred, housed, and trained under the most barbaric conditions. There are also amateur and professional levels of dogfighting, in which an increasing amount of time and money is spent to breed and train the dogs and even to provide some basic medical care for them. Recently, a fourth level of dogfighting has emerged, combining significant financial resources with street-fighting sensibilities.

Fighting dogs who will not fight or who lose fights are occasionally released, but more often than not, they are destroyed in a variety of inhumane ways: They are shot, drowned, bludgeoned, electrocuted, garroted, hung, stabbed, or, as probably happened to Oogy, given to other dogs to be torn apart. The fact that when we first met Oogy we were told that he was a pit bull suggests to me that the dealer who most likely used him for bait thought that he was a fighting dog who would not fight.

When police find fighting dogs in a raid in which they are not accompanied by the SPCA, standard procedure requires them to have the dogs transported there. The SPCA in Philadelphia told me that the Philadelphia police would not have been in Montgomery County, nor would they have taken an animal seized in a raid in

Philadelphia to a shelter in Ardmore. According to the director of operations for the Montgomery County SPCA, when police find an injured animal and call while the facility's operations are open, the animal will be brought there, where two surgeons are on call to provide emergency treatment. Given the extent of Oogy's injuries, had he been taken to that facility following the raid in which he was found, it is a virtual certainty that he would have been destroyed. The surgeons would have been faced with hours of costly procedures that, given the severity of the wounds and the myriad other medical problems they would have had to deal with, might well have proved futile. On top of that, the SPCA did not have unlimited resources to rehabilitate fighting dogs, particularly at the expense of the other animals in its care. There was no way of determining in advance whether rehabilitation efforts would be successful; after these efforts had been made, a fighting dog might still pose a threat to other animals, or even humans, in which case it could never be made available for adoption. Since time, effort, and money spent on rehabilitation attempts meant that resources would be denied to other dogs with a real likelihood of being adopted, fighting dogs almost invariably would be destroyed. The chances of a mutilated fighting dog being rehabilitated, even if it could have been saved through hours of surgery and postsurgical treatment, and then adopted were beyond remote.

At the time of Oogy's rescue, Ardmore was the only animal hospital in the immediate area to offer after-hours emergency room treatment. Had the police called the Montgomery County SPCA after hours, when the facility's operations were closed, a dispatcher would have had the authority to direct the police to take a wounded dog to Ardmore's ER. The Montgomery County SPCA has no record of that happening, and no follow-up report, which would have been generated had they directed the police there. In fact, the SPCA did not pick up or receive any fighting dogs at all on the weekend that Oogy was found. When I asked the SPCA's director of operations whether the presence of a bait dog would have necessarily meant that there had to have been fighting dogs at the site, and wondered why none had been taken to the SPCA as a result of the raid in which Oogy was found, the director told me that very often the owners "drop the dogs"—let them loose so that they will not be charged with animal cruelty. "The dogs usually turn up in a couple of days," he told me, "either as strays or when they corner somebody on the roof of their car."

I later learned that another possible reason no other fighting dogs were found in the raid is that dogs being used for street fighting are often kept at a different location from where they are fought. Since those who fight dogs are usually not concerned with providing proper care for them, the dogs are often stashed in abandoned properties so that if they are discovered, there will be no way to find the owners. And to make detection more difficult, dogfighters also regularly change the locations where they train the dogs and hold the fights.

The fact that no other dogs were found in the raid in which Oogy was discovered also suggests that Oogy may have been abandoned after he was attacked. Since there were no other animals in the house, there would have been no reason for anyone to stay there with a dying dog, especially a dog that had been abused when it was alive.

In the absence of any evidence that the Montgomery County SPCA directed that Oogy be taken to the Ardmore ER, I'm left with only one explanation as to how Oogy got to the hospital—and although it is speculative, it makes the most sense to me. I believe that Oogy was found in a local police operation, which is consistent with Dr. Bianco's recollection, and because the raid was local, the police knew about the emergency services that were available after hours through Ardmore. My best guess is that some animal-loving cop found a mutilated, dying puppy and, on his or her own initiative, brought the dog to the emergency services at Ardmore to try to save its life.

In the end, the only important thing is the fact that Oogy was discovered and brought in for treatment. I can never know why the fighting dog that attacked Oogy, and that would have been or was being trained to kill, did not in fact kill him. The emergency room services were eliminated several years after Oogy was found, and all of the ER records are gone, so I have no way of knowing if its staff ever wrote down which police department brought him in. I was told that the ER staff would probably not have bothered to note the department because it wouldn't have been relevant to treatment. I tried to locate the two doctors who had operated the ER to see what, if anything, they remembered, but I couldn't track them down. As a result, I cannot determine how the police came to learn about and raid the drug-dealing operation, or where exactly the raid occurred, or what actually happened during the raid and what was found. I can't learn the fate of any people who may have been there when the police burst in. I can never know how long Oogy lay in his cage and suffered or what that suffering consisted of. I will never know why his keepers did not kill him and put him out of his misery when they saw that the dog being trained to kill had not finished the job.

My investigation into the events that culminated in

Oogy coming to live with us also revealed that after the police rescued him, Oogy survived largely because of one woman's refusal to let him die and the efforts of a surgeon and veterinary staff who operated out of the purest of motives: to save the life of a helpless creature before them.

Diane Klein, the hospital administrator of AAH, began working with Dr. Bianco when she was just out of college, a year before he acquired the facility in 1989. The first year that the hospital was open for business, Dr. Bianco and Diane each worked one-hundred-hour weeks, yet Dr. Bianco did not generate enough income to feed his family by himself. Luckily, his wife was working at the time. For the first two years the hospital was open, Diane slept in a room on the second floor and constituted the entire staff. She worked as Dr. Bianco's assistant, managed the schedule, paid the bills, ordered supplies, kept inventory, and clipped toenails. Diane had graduated from college with a degree in biology and aspired to become a veterinarian herself. When she started with Dr. Bianco, she was taking night courses with that goal in mind. As the volume of business increased and the staff grew, in appreciation of her dedication and skills, Dr. Bianco offered to pay for Diane to get a degree in veterinary medicine. By that time, though,

Diane had married and had her first child, and she felt her time and energy were better spent focused on her family. Dr. Bianco then asked Diane to manage the office. Along the way, he also made her a partner in the business.

Both Dr. Bianco and Diane are completely committed to helping animals and will do whatever is required to achieve that end. They enjoy a professional relationship that is based on an implicit trust in each other's judgment. Ardmore Animal Hospital's national recognition reflects the professionalism and compassion that starts at the top.

"Diane loves gladiator dogs," Dr. Bianco explained to me. "But, ultimately, her generosity goes beyond this. There is no purer animal lover. She has a special affinity for dogs not given a fair shake." He paused, thought a moment, and then continued, "This business attracts a lot of people who relate better to animals than they do to humans. I've had more than one technician who rode with outlaw motorcycle gangs. I've had technicians who were literally incapable of speaking to my clients. Diane is a special blend of animal lover and people person. She is so dedicated to helping animals that she is very demanding of the staff." He smiled. "I wouldn't say the staff is afraid of her, but they certainly have a very healthy respect for her. The thing is, she is no more demanding of the staff than she is of herself."

By her own admission, Diane would make a lousy animal rights advocate. "It must be the Italian in me. I have no tolerance for people who abuse animals. I'm not capable of reasoning with them. I couldn't deal with these people rationally. But then, there's nothing rational about them." She laughed. "I'd go after them with a hammer."

Monday, December 16, 2002, was the second anniversary of the death of Diane's all-time favorite dog, Maddie, a Staffordshire terrier–bulldog mix that had been with Diane for thirteen years, ultimately succumbing to cancer. The night before, she and her husband had looked at some videos of the dog. At first, they had laughed at Maddie's antics, but eventually their sense of loss overcame them, and they had cried and comforted each other. On the drive to work that Monday morning, Diane was unable to stop thinking of Maddie, remembering favorite moments. She felt down, a bit distracted.

Diane turned onto the quiet, tree-lined street where the hospital is located in an old Victorian-style home. At the time, AAH carried a staff of six doctors and eight to ten technicians. The hospital also offered the services of two animal specialists one night a week. In addition, AAH leased its facilities and equipment to an after-hours and weekend emergency service owned and operated by two doctors who utilized the hospital's facilities but were not on staff.

Diane parked behind the hospital. As she did every morning, she came in through the back door, and as she did every morning, the first place she went was the treatment room, where hospitalized and surgical cases were housed, to see if any animals had come in through the ER.

The room was painted in hues of beige and brick and smelled like isopropyl alcohol and adhesive tape. Against the far wall from the entrance were two tiers of three small cages sitting on top of two larger cages. Additional cages lined the two walls on either side; an oxygen cage also sat to the right of the entrance to the room. The bottom of each cage was carpeted with shredded newspaper and had built-in dishes for water and food. Medical instruments were stocked in the drawers of a stainless-steel examination table that stood in the center of the room.

The first thing Diane saw as she entered the room was a white pup lying in one of the small cages against the opposite wall. His head was on the floor between his paws. The left half of his skull was swathed in white gauze stained with blood, held in place by adhesive tape. The pup's body was spotted with dark, dried blood. Bloody, pus-filled holes and gashes covered the side of his face and the part of his skull not obscured by the bandage. Diane began to seethe as it became apparent to her that the ER had basically done nothing for the poor animal. They had not even bothered to clean off his blood. As soon as Diane walked into the room, the pup lifted his head and his right ear stood at attention; his large, dark eyes looked at her, and she couldn't take her eyes off him. As she stood there transfixed, the dog struggled to his feet, sneezed, and shook his head. Blood droplets sprayed from under the bandage. Then, incredibly, he started to wag his tail.

Diane walked over to the cage past one of the ER physicians, who was standing in the room focusing on some sort of paperwork. She bent and stared at the pup, her nose only inches from his. The pup appeared to be a pit bull or a pit bull mix, but it was difficult to tell exactly because of his swollen and distorted head. Diane's thoughts slipped to Maddie, then returned to the pup in front of her. She straightened, her eyes never leaving the dog. She pointed to the animal and, without averting her gaze, asked the doctor, "What the *hell* is *that*?"

Somewhat startled, the doctor looked up to see what Diane was talking about and then told her that the dog had been found following a raid and likely had been used as bait. He explained that the police had brought the dog over to the ER for treatment.

The dog sat back down and looked at Diane. The nostrils of his large black nose twitched at Diane's proximity. The three-by-five-inch cage card read "Male Pit Bull or PB Mix" and showed December 15 as the date of admission. The dog's age was estimated at three to four months on the cage card, but Diane thought that estimate was high. Looking through the chart, she saw that, in addition to the visible wounds on his head, the left ear and much of the left side of the dog's face was gone, torn off by the violence that had been inflicted upon him. Diane was astonished by the fact that the pup did not exhibit any signs of the constant, staggering pain she knew he must have been experiencing. She was also amazed by the fact that after what had happened to him, he didn't seem to be afraid of her. He simply continued to sit in the cage and watch her calmly.

There was untouched food in the cage. The ER staff had cleaned the largest wound on the left side of the pup's face, given the dog an injection of steroids to counteract shock, and injected him with antibiotics. They had not given him any blood or tried substantively to treat his injuries. The ER staff were not doing what Diane refers to as "above and beyond." They had expended only the minimal effort needed to keep him alive. No one owned the dog, so there was no one to hold the ER accountable for his treatment or to pay for the effort that it would take to try to repair the damage he had suffered. As a result, Diane learned, the doctor planned on transferring the dog to the SPCA.

From experience, she knew that if the pup was transferred to the SPCA, he would be euthanized.

Aware that the doctor's likely plans for the pup would lead to his destruction, moved by what he had already endured and his sweet, calm demeanor, and well aware of the magnitude of the fight that lay ahead, Diane asked if the doctor would sign over the animal to her. She wanted to at least make an effort to save the dog's life. The doctor agreed, because once the transfer had occurred, the dog's welfare was no longer his responsibility.

Dr. Bianco was upstairs in his office doing paperwork. When he came down to the first floor to begin his day's rounds, Diane immediately went over to him, the words spilling out of her.

"I need your help," she said to him. "Will you take a look at this dog who came in over the weekend? He was used as a bait dog. Half his face is missing. The police brought him in and the ER doctor was going to send him to the SPCA, so I had him signed over to me. The SPCA will just destroy him. I want to try to save him. He's really cute and seems very sweet, and I really feel badly for him."

Dr. Bianco looked at her and shook his head in mock

disbelief. "Oh God, Diane…" He sighed. "Not another one." Then he smiled and said, "Okay. Let's go have a look."

Dr. Bianco followed Diane back into the treatment room, where he pulled on a pair of latex gloves and opened the door to the dog's cage. He lifted him out and placed him on the examination table. Cradling the dog's head in his left arm to immobilize him, Dr. Bianco took a scissors from one of the drawers and cut open the bandage. With his right foot, he pressed the pedal that opened the top of the medical waste bin on the floor at the end of the examination table and dumped the bloody wad of gauze and tape into it. Saturated with and stiffened by discharge from the dog's wounds, the bandage landed with a loud thump, as though it were made out of plaster of Paris. With his right hand, Dr. Bianco stroked the dog's flank to calm him down and erase his fear. The pup offered absolutely no resistance. Dr. Bianco, too, was astonished that despite everything that had happened to him, and despite the way humans had so obviously mistreated him, the dog exhibited no signs of anxiety. He seemed to understand somehow that the people around him now were different from those who had controlled his life before; that they were kind, even though he had probably never before experienced human kindness.

The pup's ribs were prominent, which told Dr. Bianco that he was malnourished. His breathing was shallow, but he did not open his mouth for additional air, which was a sign of distress. His head and neck were caked with iodine brown dried blood. His features were horrifically damaged. There were multiple infected puncture wounds on the right side of his face and skull. The left side of his face and forehead were gone. What had been that side of his face, from just back of his muzzle to behind where his ear used to be, was now yellow green pus, oozing blood, and fully infected. All that remained of his left ear was a jagged stump. The tissue surrounding the yawning cavity where the left side of the pup's face had been was dead and blackened; the rotted flesh smelled like meat that had been left out in the sun for days. The blood vessels on that side of his forehead had been torn apart. And yet, incredibly, although he had to have been in tremendous pain, he gave no indication of it.

Based on the conditions he observed and the extent of ruin and infection he found, Dr. Bianco estimated that the dog had been lying untreated and unattended for five to seven days. He did not want to contemplate what the pup had endured during that period. Despite the fact that the pup had been losing blood the entire time, the ER doctors had not done a blood count or given him any transfusions. In his weakened state, the dog would surely have a difficult time surviving both the extensive infection and the shock of surgical trauma if Dr. Bianco were to operate, and operating offered the only chance of saving the dog's life.

Dr. Bianco gently removed his elbow and laid the pup's head down on the table. The dog lay on his side, exhausted; his tail swatted feebly several times. Dr. Bianco rubbed the dog's neck. Even with the pup's face so swollen and mutilated, Diane thought that he was undeniably cute. She gently touched the top of the dog's head and bent over him, her eyes on Dr. Bianco's face.

Dr. Bianco looked back at Diane. He shook his head in the negative and shrugged. He pursed his lips grimly, then said, "Diane, I'm sorry. I don't think I can save this dog."

Diane straightened from where she had been crouched over the pup. She looked into Dr. Bianco's eyes. "Dr. Bianco," she said. "You've *got* to save this dog."

Dr. Bianco's father and his uncles had all been craftsmen who worked with their hands. They were stonemasons, welders, and carpenters who had always taken great pride in what they created for the use of others. Dr. Bianco credits them with having given him the manual dexterity to be an exceptionally effective surgeon. With no other reason than the fact that helpless before him lay a victim of horrific abuse that might possibly be saved, and moved by Diane's determination that every effort be made to preserve this life, Dr. Bianco started surgery.

The operation lasted several hours. First, Dr. Bianco's assistant gave the dog general anesthesia. Dr. Bianco then started him on an antibiotic treatment and flushed the hole where his face had been to clean the gaping wound. He cut away the dead tissue and inserted a Penrose drain into the exposed portion of the animal's face, a plastic tube that came out through an opening Dr. Bianco made in the underside of the jaw. This would allow blood and other fluids to escape, to prevent infection and promote proper healing. After this, he sutured the gaping meat that the dog's face had become. They transfused blood and liquid nourishment into the dog intravenously.

The dog survived the surgery.

He wasn't Oogy then. In fact, he didn't have a name. For superstitious reasons, the staff didn't name animals whom they didn't know and didn't expect to survive. By all rights, this dog should have been nothing more than one of the uncountable number whose lives are lost or destroyed as the result of dogfighting each year. Yet even though the pup had no real prospects for survival, the hospital staff worked together to do everything they could to save him. No one would be there to thank them if they were successful, and there was no one to pay for all the time and effort they were putting in. There was no guarantee that they would accomplish their goal or, if they did, whether the dog would be able to establish a successful, loving relationship with a human or another animal. But they persevered. Their efforts were, in the truest sense, simply a collective exercise in the right thing to do.

The surgery was over, but the dog wasn't out of the woods: The hospital team soon discovered that their patient would not eat. He would occasionally take a little soft food, but not the quantity that he needed in order to regain his strength; neither did he offer any visual or behavioral clues as to what was interfering with his ability to eat. Dr. Bianco did not know if it was an internal complication or something else. Bloodwork gave no indication of infection. There was a fistula just below where the pup's left ear had been. Dr. Bianco simply had a gut feeling as to what he needed to do next. He reached into the jaw with a forceps and felt loose bone. He extracted a piece of the dog's jawbone about the shape and size of a fifty-cent piece. A section of the dog's lower mandible had been broken off and had been digging into the roof of his mouth whenever he bit down, sending a lightning bolt of pain through his being. He had been in such extensive discomfort that he could not functionally operate his mouth, but he had never showed this. His threshold for pain was extraordinary.

The forty-five-minute procedure to remove the shattered bone enabled the dog to eat again. He began to take solid food on a regular basis and started to gain strength and to put on weight.

Dr. Bianco was in awe of the power of the beast that had inflicted the wounds with which he had had to contend. The dog that had grabbed this pup had a bite forceful enough not just to fracture, but to break off a piece of his jaw. Dr. Bianco had attended seminars given by humane societies and rescue centers to teach veterinarians how to recognize injuries associated with dogfighting. As part of this training, he had seen films of actual fights, and he could easily imagine the scene that culminated in the devastating injuries the pup had suffered. The fighting dog would have grabbed the pup, which would have been howling and bawling and squealing in pain and terror the entire time, and shaken him like a rag, slamming him into the floor, slamming him into the side of the cage had they been in a box. It was nothing short of a miracle, given the pup's malnourished state, that he had survived the attack at all. To have also survived the subsequent prolonged period of suffering and inattention, the loss of blood and extensive infection, the absence of food and water, and then the surgical trauma was, in Dr. Bianco's estimation and experience, truly miraculous.

Diane had been aware of all of this, too. Dr. Bianco knew that Diane had had an almost visceral response to what this dog had endured and that her determination to save the dog was in direct proportion to the extent that she sensed he had suffered. She did not want him to die, and she would not let him. She had saved the dog from certain euthanasia and then set in motion the process to provide some semblance of normality in the dog's life.

For Oogy to have survived all of this certainly suggests that he had to have been fighting to stay alive. But based on what his life had been up to that point, what would have driven that determination? I want to believe that he sensed there was something better waiting for him.

Trauma is easier to overcome than long-term maltreatment, because abuse becomes a way of life and affects the dog's spirits. Although the pup had suffered both trauma and abuse, because he was so young and neither had been prolonged, neither seemed to have had a permanent effect on him. He continued to heal and then began to flourish. His condition and the cruelty he had endured produced a heartfelt, deeply caring reaction among the hospital staff. His happy, affectionate nature was seemingly more pronounced because of the horror he had undergone. They warmed to him. As Diane described it, "He became everybody's dog." The entire staff participated in caring for the dog and nurturing him. Buoyant with optimism, after another ten days Diane took him home to begin fostering him for adoption.

She named him Eli because he was white, which made her think of a cotton ball, which led her to Eli Whitney, the inventor of the cotton gin. She wanted to keep him, but her own dog was jealous.

"He was just another white pit bull as far as I was concerned," Dr. Bianco later told me. "But he had a charming personality. You have to understand that we get pit bulls in here on a somewhat regular basis. We repair them when we can and try to adopt them out. There's dogfighting going on in this area. One time a kid brought in a pit bull he said had been attacked. He was crying, and he said he could not afford the surgery. One of my clients, who was in the waiting room when the kid came in, volunteered to pay for it. The surgery cost her eight hundred dollars. Several months later, the kid came back with the dog torn up again. He was clearly fighting the dog. I confronted him. I said to him, 'You're fighting this dog.' He denied it, of course. I told him, 'Listen, I know you are. I'll fix him up this time, but don't bring him back here again.'"

The Pennsylvania SPCA, which is located in Philadelphia, receives anywhere from fifty to seventy-five reports of dogfighting a month. Through the years, I have met fighting dogs that have survived and other rescued dogs that have been abused and mistreated in horrific fashion. But for obvious reasons, survival is exceedingly rare in a dog who has been used as bait and mutilated to the extent that

Oogy had been. And it's even rarer that, after the unspeakable depravity and abuse that had been inflicted upon him, the dog maintained a trusting, loving spirit.

I am routinely overwhelmed by the circumstances that brought Oogy to us. There are so many "ifs" involved: if the fighting dog had killed Oogy as he was supposed to do; if Oogy had not somehow survived his torment; if the police had not raided the facility at the moment they did; if the raid had not been local, so that the police would not have had access to ER services; if Diane and Dr. Bianco and the staff had not been so determined to save Oogy...

Long after Oogy had come to live with us, when I had pieced together as best I could how events had unfolded, I related the story to Noah and Dan, told them how Diane had refused to allow Oogy to be sent to the SPCA, insisted that Dr. Bianco save him, and had essentially dedicated herself to not letting him die.

Noah blurted out, amazed, "Really? That really happened? Diane really did that?" He broke into a wide grin. "Jeez," he said. "Diane's a freakin' saint!"

"Saint Diane!" Dan exclaimed. "I like that." He rolled it around in his thoughts for a few seconds. "Saint Diane," he said. He, too, had a broad smile on his face. "The patron saint of hopeless causes."

CHAPTER 3 *The Stork*

the boys have always known they were adopted. They were three days old when they came into our lives, and we told them the very first day how ecstatic we were with the way events had played out. Even before they could acknowledge it, they were told how they came to be in our house and made it incandescent. It is nothing we ever hid from them. It is part of who they are.

Perhaps this explains why, when the boys were very young, one of their favorite stories was how the pets they shared the house with then, a rescued dog and two rescued cats, came to be in our family. I think that knowing how beloved these animals were, being able to love them on their own, and the story of how all of this came to be reassured them that kindness and caring are neither limited nor determined by the traditional biological parent-child relationship. What matters are the opportunities that are created and the extent to which the offered potential is fulfilled—the chance and ability to give love and support when they are most needed.

I would be flattering myself if I said that I'd been ambivalent about becoming a father. Nothing about parenting had generated any eagerness in me, no doubt as a result of the attenuated relationship I had had with my own parents and the experiences of my own childhood. However, because Jennifer badly wanted to be a mother, I agreed to pursue the choice. We endured multiple miscarriages, faced fertility issues, and ultimately gave up trying to get pregnant. We looked at several adoption agencies, but because I was over forty we did not satisfy their criteria. Ultimately, a friend told us about Golden Cradle, an adoption agency located in south New Jersey that did not consider age a determinative factor in one's ability to be a good parent. We applied and were accepted into the program.

Arty Elgart had founded Golden Cradle, which is a nonprofit organization, after it took him five years to adopt his first child. Arty had concluded that adoption should not have to be such an arduous experience, and he sought to expedite the process of matching would-be parents with birth parents. After fifteen years on the

Golden Cradle board of directors, I have come to the conclusion that what has made traditional Golden Cradle adoptions so successful—those in which the agency finds and assists the birth parent(s) and then arranges for the adoption by parents in the program, who have paid a fee—is that the agency makes certain that an adoption happens for the right reasons. There is no lingering regret by the birth mother or birth parents; they understand that it is in the best interests of the child to place him or her in the hands of another couple. There is no second-guessing; they know the child will be well loved and that they are sharing a gift of inestimable value.

In a traditional adoption, the birth parents pick the parents to whom the child is going to be introduced. When an expectant mother or couple who wanted to place their child for adoption through Golden Cradle contacted the agency, Golden Cradle would focus on what was important to the birth mother or birth parents. The agency would ask, What characteristics do you want to see in the couple who will adopt your child? And if the mother answered, Well, I'm Italian, and I am a potter, so I'd like the child's parents to be Italian professionals interested in the arts, Golden Cradle would reply, Well, we have an Italian couple who are not professional and are not really interested in the arts, and we have a Jewish professional couple who are. What's more important to you, religion or lifestyle? Depending upon the responses that Golden Cradle received to the questions posed, it provided prospective adoptive couples' autobiographies for the birth parents or birth mother to choose from that reflected the birth parents' interests.

For the first six months after placement had occurred, adoptive parents would prepare what were known as "Sharing Sheets," letting the birth mother/parents know how the child was developing and the parent-child relationships were evolving. The Sharing Sheets, each of which included at least six photographs, were turned over to Golden Cradle and forwarded to the birth parent(s). Knowing that the child was doing well and was loved and appreciated served to confirm the correctness of the decision and helped the birth parent(s) to say good-bye.

When we joined Golden Cradle, forty couples at a time were accepted into the program, all of whom were waiting for children through traditional adoptions. Arty spoke at the first meeting of our class. And the first thing he said was: "I want you all to relax. You're all going to be parents. One couple has to be first, and one couple has to be last, but you're all going to get a baby."

Early on, Golden Cradle staffers had learned that when they called adoptive parents for administrative reasons and told them, "This is Golden Cradle," people would flip out, thinking that they had just been placed and were now parents. So at the first meeting everyone was informed that if someone called and said they were from Golden Cradle, it did *not* mean there was a baby waiting for them. When the phone rang and the voice on the other end said, "This is the stork calling," the baby was there.

Jennifer and I ended up being the last in our class to be placed. It took almost two years. We had been waiting for the call so long, we had stopped thinking about it. Despite the assurances we had received, it seemed a distant possibility, not guaranteed or inevitable. Anticipation about becoming parents had long since faded into the grind of our daily lives. We stopped wondering about and planning for a future centered around kids. As it turned out, twice before we actually were placed, birth mothers had picked us before changing their minds about placing their children. Hence, no "stork call." But we had no way of knowing that at the time. And as things turned out, it all was for the best.

I was forty-four years old when we got our stork call. In retrospect, I am glad this part of my life came as a complete surprise. If somebody had said to me ahead of time, "You're going to be the forty-four-year-old father of twins," I would have said, "There's no *way* that's going to happen." I was riddled with doubts as to my ability to be an effective father. I felt wholly inadequate and unprepared to be the father of one child, let alone two at the same time.

One Saturday morning, Jenny and I were sitting on the couch having coffee, reading the paper, and getting ready to go into center city and put in a few hours at our respective law firms. I had come to believe that some people consume themselves with their jobs and careers so that they do not have the time to examine the emptiness or unhappiness in their lives. I think we were like that. We were both under enormous pressure to perform, and neither of us had the confidence to feel that we were good enough, which kept us working harder, pushing a burden up-slope to a destination we could never reach. We had substituted work for a life of substantive content and meaning. We were simply going through the motions.

And then the telephone rang.

Jennifer and I looked at each other. Neither of us had any idea who might be at the other end of the line. It wasn't the time of day that the phone rang in our house. My first reaction to phone calls at unexpected hours was that they bore bad news. I stood up, put the section of the newspaper I had been reading on the couch, the coffee cup on the end table. I walked to the bookcase and picked up the receiver.

"Good morning," I said, trying to sound as positive as

I could. I would defy the intruder on the other end of the line.

"Hello, Larry. It's Susan from Golden Cradle. Guess what? This is your stork call."

Susan was the social worker we had worked with since enrolling with Golden Cradle. My thoughts immediately went to the night before. Every Friday night for years, a bunch of us from the office had gone out to a bar. I sensed in that moment that I would never again go out drinking with the folks I worked with. I never did.

I felt as if I had been hit in the back of the head with a two-by-four, except that it didn't hurt. Everything had been knocked out of me. It was our social worker, Susan, telling me that we were parents. What did *that* mean?

Rather stunned, I said the first thing that came into my head: "Really? That's amazing." I was buying time, trying to internalize what Susan had just told me.

Susan said, "Congratulations. You and Jen are parents. Would you like to know what you have?"

"Of course," I said.

"You've got a boy," Susan said. "He's three days old and he's absolutely beautiful."

"No kidding!" I exclaimed. I had the strangest feeling, as though I were speaking under water. "I guess this means," I said, "that we don't get to go to the movies tonight, right?"

By now, Jennifer had put down her newspaper and was looking at me, trying to figure out what was going on.

"Wait," Susan said. "There's more."

"There's more?" I asked. I was in a complete state of shock as it was. "What do you mean, there's more?"

And Susan said, "Your son has a brother. You've got *twins!*"

"Here," I said, suddenly overwhelmed by this news, and held out the receiver to Jennifer. I realized that everything in my life had abruptly been reprioritized. Concerns I could never have been able to imagine would from now on take precedence and control my days. I recalled, in some remote part of my brain, a conversation I had had with my oldest friend, who found out at forty that she was pregnant with twins. In typical fashion for her, she had researched the parenting experience. She had told me that the studies showed that if you were parenting correctly, you would not have time for many of the things that you thought were important before you became a parent, but you would feel more fulfilled as a result. I'd had no idea what she meant. At the time she told me this, my hobby was photography, and I was working in my darkroom twice a week until 2:00 or 3:00 in the morning. I could not imagine giving that up. I have spent a total of two nights in the darkroom since the boys came home, printing up photos as a favor to a friend. I have never once missed it.

"Congratulations," I informed Jennifer. "You're a mom." Then I added, "It's twins."

I hope that I was smiling as I said this, but I really can't remember. Jennifer shrieked, "What?!" and jumped off the couch as though she had received an electric shock. She grabbed the receiver and started talking to Susan. I mentally drifted away, trying to absorb the information and figure out the next step. At some point Jennifer began to cry. If I recall correctly, she did not stop crying for at least two days.

Finally, Jennifer hung up the phone. Mascara colored her face beneath her eyes like an athlete's eye black. "They said we can show up anytime after twelve," she told me, sniffling. "The birth mother is still there. She needs some time to say good-bye."

I nodded, pursing my lips. "That's understandable," I said.

We realized that we needed to get dressed and go to a baby store. We had absolutely nothing in the house for a baby, because in Jewish tradition the *keinahora* says that it is bad luck if you plan for a baby before it arrives. All we had was a room on the second floor painted dark yellow, which was where the baby (one!) was to go, and which held only a tan couch, a set of curtains and a window shade for each of the two windows, and three bare white bookshelves anchored into the wall. We had no baby clothing, no formula, no bedding; we had no books, no toys. There were no bottles, no cribs, and no dressers. We did not have a name for one baby, let alone for two. We had nothing. We were completely unprepared for this. We hugged each other and went upstairs to get dressed.

I put on my tuxedo. How often would I get to be a father and bring two boys home? I wore bright red socks and my black sneakers so people would know that on some level, at least, I wasn't taking myself too seriously. In later years, the boys admitted that they were very impressed to learn that I treated the event with such significance that I went to the trouble of wearing a tuxedo (even paired with red socks) in order to go meet them for the first time. The tux was a hand-me-down from my dad, whom it no longer fit. Somewhere in there, a circle was being completed, but I didn't have time to think about this. We called Jennifer's parents in Bethesda to tell them the news; they said they would pack and arrive later in the afternoon. My own parents were out, so we were not able to tell them yet that they had finally become grandparents. We called our siblings, scattered around the country. We called some friends. We asked people to spread the word that the next day we would have everyone over for an open house. Jennifer called a caterer to arrange for food to be delivered. The real estate agent who had sold us our house, and who had become a friend, ordered two stork signs for us to plant on the lawn to announce the boys' arrival.

We drove to the closest available baby store. Jennifer went to look at furniture. I explained to the saleswoman who approached me that we had two newborn boys coming into our house and had absolutely nothing for them but an empty room.

"Congratulations," she said. "You're on the way to pick them up now?"

I nodded. "In an hour," I told her.

"Well, to start with, you'll need car seats," she pointed out.

She walked me over to a little room off the main part of the store, took a gray plastic car seat off a shelf, and set it on the floor. The inside of the shell contained a padded cushion; a belt and two straps were joined at the center buckle.

"Can you show me how to use that?" I asked.

"Of course." She knelt next to the car seat. She turned it over and showed me where the car's seat belt slid through the bottom of the carrier assembly to hold it in place on the seat. Next, she demonstrated how the carrier locked into place on its base when the lever was pushed down and how it disengaged when the handle was flipped back. The handle that locked the seat into place in the car was used to carry the child when the seat was disengaged. She cautioned me that the carriers were to be placed on the rear seat facing toward the back of the car. Then she turned the carrier around and started explaining to me how to place the child in and restrain him. But nothing she said seemed to take.

"I'm sorry," I apologized. "I'm having a hard time following how this works. Can you show me?" I reached around her and picked up a stuffed animal, a little gray-and-white elephant. I handed the elephant to her to use as a visual demonstration. I needed to see what I needed to do.

"Okay," she said. "First you open the harness like this." She pressed the center button on the buckle, which released the shoulder straps. The buckle itself was on a strap located on the bottom of the seat. "Then you place your baby in the seat like this." She looked up at me to see if I was watching her, then turned her face downward again to concentrate on what she was doing. She put the elephant in the car seat and pulled the buckle up to its chest from between its legs. "You move his little trunk out of the way like so, then slide the clasp back into place." She lifted the elephant's short trunk and pushed the clasp for the shoulder straps into the buckle until it clicked into place. She looked up again with a smile.

"Voilà," she said, raising both hands in a gesture of triumph.

I bought the elephant, too. It was the boys' first toy. They still have it. I hope that they always will.

We also bought two cribs with mattresses, four sets of sheets, four blankets, and four pillowcases. We purchased several boxes of formula, bottles and bottle liners, clothes, and some more toys. Jennifer ordered a dresser that would be delivered in a couple of days. We bought wipes, diapers, and talcum powder, just enough of what we needed to get started and until we could figure out where it was cheapest to get more. We managed to fit all of this into the trunk of the car. Then we made the twenty-minute drive to Cherry Hill.

We entered the building where the Golden Cradle offices were located and took the elevator to the agency's suite. Because this was the first set of twins at Golden Cradle in five years, the entire staff had gathered in celebration. Everyone accompanied us into the conference room, offered their heartfelt congratulations, and then left us there, closing the door. Alone together, Jennifer and I clasped hands. We were about to experience one of those moments in life for which there can be no dress rehearsal. We stood staring at the door that had just been closed behind us. What *was* behind door number one?

There was a soft knock and the door opened. Shelly,

a social worker who assisted with birth parents and who had flown out to meet and return with the boys and their mother, came in with the babies, one cradled in each arm. The boys were wrapped in white blankets festooned with yellow stars. Shelly was grinning from ear to ear; just about five feet tall, with red hair, she reminded me of a leprechaun.

"Here," she said. She handed one of the boys to Jennifer. "One for *you*," she said, and turned, handed me the other boy, and said, "and one for *you*."

Then she left, closing the door softly behind her, and the staff left the four of us alone for twenty minutes.

I had never before held a newborn child. He was sleeping. It felt as if I were holding a pillow.

The first thing I said to Jennifer was, "Oh, my goodness."

The boy I was holding had a tiny, wrinkled red face that was so pushed in it looked as if it had been hit by a shovel. His hands appeared shriveled, like little monkey hands. I looked at the boy Jennifer was holding, and he looked exactly the same way. I said, "They're really funny-looking. I think they look like ET."

"Trust me," Jennifer said. Her mascara was streaming down her face again. "They're beautiful."

I had no idea how she could tell that, but she proved to be right.

I was not sure what we should do next. They were asleep, so there was no sense in rocking them.

"Okay," I said to the one I was holding. "Who are you?"

There was not a lot of talking to be done. We were simply awestruck at the sudden sequence of events. We sat on the couch and placed the boys between us and stared at them. Then we switched boys. After that, we each experienced holding both of them. We must have used the word *amazing* eight times. They did not open their eyes, so we had no idea what color they were. They did not wake up. It was inconceivable to imagine the power they now held over us. And there had been a subtle but critically important change within me, although I was not to realize it for years to come. I was no longer afraid of being a father—now I was afraid of not being a good one.

Then Susan and the agency's director returned to fill us in on the boys' family history. A brother of theirs, who was three years older than our boys, had been adopted when he was several weeks old and was living in New England.

This time, the birth parents had contacted Golden Cradle three days before the due date to arrange for adoption. At the time they contacted Golden Cradle, however, they did not know that they were about to become the

61

parents of twins. In the sonograms, one of the boys was in front of or on top of the other, and no one appeared to have paid much attention to what was really going on in there. After the first boy was born, we were told, their mother said, "I don't think I'm done yet." She was rushed into surgery, and the second boy was delivered by C-section twenty minutes after she had delivered the first.

We also learned that the birth parents initially asked for the twins to be placed with their brother in New England, but the couple who had adopted the boys' brother responded that they were not in a position to adopt twins. Shelly discussed other adoption possibilities with the birth parents, then flew to their home state a day before the births occurred with the files of several prospective adoptive couples in whom the birth parents had expressed interest. Then, after we were selected, and after the twins had been delivered, Shelly had to scramble to call Golden Cradle to see if Jennifer and I had preapproved twins. The agency would not place twins separately and would place them only with a couple who had agreed ahead of time that they would accept multiple siblings in the event that occurred.

We had been fascinated with the notion of twins for years, ever since an old friend of mine had visited with his three-month-old twin sons. Watching their similarities and the way they interacted with one another even at so young an age revealed a special bond that seemed to add another dimension to their relationship with each other as well as with the overall family dynamic. As a result, we had preapproved twins, but we had never expected that the adoption process would yield such a result.

On the way out of Golden Cradle that morning, Susan gave us a black-and-white copy of a photograph of the boys' older brother at six months.

"Here," she said. "This will give you some idea of what your sons are going to look like."

As it turned out, it really didn't. Their brother has dark hair and dark skin. Noah and Dan are strawberry blonds. Both are taller than their brother. The three do share gray green eyes, however, and similar builds, lean and muscular.

The boys' birth mother had flown with them to Golden Cradle and was still there the day we went to pick them up so that she could nurse them until the surrender occurred. She wanted to make sure that she would give them the best possible start in life. We were told that when she was leaving, she looked at them for the last time and said, "These boys are Levins."

Our visit to Golden Cradle lasted about an hour and a half, and at some point someone took a picture of me sitting on the couch with both boys on my lap. I look stunned. My eyes appear murky, unfocused, as though I had not slept in days. Perhaps I was beginning to crash from the adrenaline rush of the preceding several hours. I had never been jacked that high before, and I could not have had any idea what all of this would come to mean.

On the way over to Golden Cradle that morning, Jennifer and I, for the first time, had begun tossing around possible names. It was kind of like buying a house, involving lots of trial and error until we both could agree on something. We knew we both had to agree, because the results of the decision would be permanent. Very quickly we happily settled on Noah as the name of the firstborn. This was an easy choice because the boys had come two by two. Then, once we had agreed on Noah as the name for boy number one, we agreed that the second boy should also have a biblical first name. That second name proved more difficult to decide upon. Over the next several days, we tried out different names one after the other—Aaron, Adam, Ari, Benjamin, Caleb, David, Eli, Ezekiel, Gabriel, Gideon, Isaiah, Jonah—but we were unable to agree on a name for our second son. None of them seemed to fit with Levin. Until we agreed on a second name, the boys were "Baby One" and "Baby Two" by order of birth. Finally, we settled on Daniel for the younger boy. We could not recall a single Dan we had ever known who was not a stand-up guy. Dan's middle name, Garrett (which for several of his early years he thought was "Carrot"), was for his maternal grandfather, Gershon. In Jewish tradition, one uses the initial of a deceased person and not the name. Noah was initially Noah Alexander, for no other reason than it sounded nice.

One of the ironies in all this is that the day we received the stork call from Golden Cradle, my dad had gone to the emergency room with severe stomach pains, which is why my parents had not been at home when we called to tell them that they were finally grandparents. These stomach pains proved to be the precursor of the cancer that killed him four months later. He did not get to enjoy our boys for long, but at least when he died he knew he was a grandfather. As the boys' adoptions had not been finalized at the time of my father's death, we changed Noah's middle name to Harte, for Herbert, my dad's first name.

In their infancy, we color-coded everything in order to distinguish what belonged to whom. All of Noah's bottles had red dots appended to them. Dan's bottles had blue dots. Noah had the red blanket and the red socks, Dan the blue. We never dressed them alike. We always made it a point to stress their individuality.

During the first six months, there might have been an hour out of every twenty-four, if we were lucky, in which both boys were asleep at the same time. As a result,

Jennifer and I were constantly and completely exhausted. In fact, we were barely functioning. I would sleep from just after dinner until 2:00 or 3:00 a.m., when Jennifer would awaken me and I would take over while she went to sleep until 7:00 or 8:00 a.m., when I would shower and dress and stumble to work. When I came home, I would fall asleep on the floor or wherever I happened to be when I could no longer stay awake, while whoever was in the house took no notice and walked around me as if I were simply another piece of furniture. The boys' ability to sleep for extended periods gradually increased, but it was not until they were almost three years old that both of them slept through the night on a regular basis. Until then, whichever one of us could manage to get up and respond to whichever one of them was awake did so.

Jennifer's parents came up from Maryland to help as often as they could, usually every other week. Before my dad died, he and my mom visited on three or four occasions, but under the circumstances, there was no assumption of responsibility for the lives of the boys as there was with Jennifer's parents. Other relatives of mine would also drop by periodically, my closest aunt and uncle, Esther and Bernie, the most often, and they were also the most help next to Jennifer's parents. After my father died, my mom would come by for very short visits—she would stay longer if other family members were there, for dinner, say—sometimes only for ten minutes, "to see how the boys were doing." She could not stay away, but she also made it clear that she did not feel comfortable in our home, as though it were an imposition.

We went through enough diapers to warrant our own landfill. There were regular sorties for diapers, formula, and, when they had outgrown the need for formula, juice. We spent many Friday and Saturday nights over the next two years shopping. In fact, shopping pretty much came to define the way we spent our weekends. One evening at the market when I was buying juice and diapers, as I stood in front of the cashier, I started laughing out loud. The checkout girl looked at me, puzzled. "In one end and out the other," I explained. She did not see the humor in this.

Seeing newborn twins, total strangers wondered regularly about the birthing experience; time and time again, their temerity in asking personal questions amazed us. It was never easy explaining to people we did not know and would never see again what it was like to be the parents of twins when they would not have had any reason to suspect that we were not the birth parents. For example, because Jennifer is so petite, it was not unusual for another mother to comment, "But you're so small! Was it hard having twins?" "No," Jennifer would answer. "It wasn't." People we had never met before asked Jennifer how she had lost the weight so quickly. "It wasn't really a problem for me," she would respond serenely. We decided very early on that it was no business of strangers that the boys were adopted; that was something they could tell people if they wanted to. Initially, I had felt some urge to tell people, which I now think represented some attempt to distance myself from fatherhood. But as time passed, and the overwhelming experience proved to be one of joy and marvel at the bounty with which we had been blessed, my reluctance, born of the fear of failure, faded. The very labor of nurturing paid immeasurable dividends, and after several months, after my head had stopped whirling at what had happened and I had accepted it as part of my life, I became their father, and all our lives were joined. There was nothing to distinguish me from them.

Watching their personalities emerge was a constantly rewarding experience. They were home for only a few weeks before they earned nicknames. Noah became "the Professor" because he was so contemplative. He seemed constantly to look at things as though he were trying to figure out what they were, what they were supposed to do, and how they went about doing exactly whatever it was they were supposed to accomplish. Dan was nick-named "Jarhead" because of his bald, round dome and absolute determination, his commanding sense of bravado.

The first time I heard the boys giggling uncontrollably, I sensed that it was a sound I had never heard before or made. As it turned out, everything about the way the boys grew up would be different from my own childhood experiences.

When I was three years old, my sister, Susie, died of leukemia. She was two years older than me, three years younger than my brother. I have only two memories of her.

One is of our father holding her in his arms in the alley behind our house, on a block of semidetached houses in West Philadelphia. It is a hot summer day, and our dad is using a handkerchief to shoo away a yellow jacket that has been buzzing around Susie and frightening her. She is crying, and he is speaking soothingly to her. Since in reality he proved to be powerless to protect her, I guess that it is understandable why I hold on to this.

Susie is not present in the only other memory I have of her. She is in the hospital, dying. She may already have died. It is a Sunday morning. My parents and I, accompanied by my aunt Esther, have driven to the hospital from our house. Another aunt is home with my brother. The car is suffused with an aura of grim resignation; there is only one inevitable conclusion to the events of the morning. I am too young to be admitted to the hospital, so I sit outside in the car alone. I do not to this day understand why my parents even brought me. I remember a black steel fence and a massive yellow brick building visible from where the car was parked on the street. I remember Aunt Esther coming to the car, dabbing at her eyes with a tissue, to say that Susie had died.

In the house I grew up in, there was only one picture of Susie to be found—just one picture for as long as we owned the house, which was another twenty-three years. It sat on the piano along with a number of other photos of different family members, events, gatherings, and occasions. This one photograph showed a beaming little face with dimples and two long, golden braids. I would look at the picture for minutes at a time, trying to get to know the girl in it, but it never felt like anything more than a picture. The little girl had been my sister, but the photograph could have been of anyone. There was no connection.

My parents seem to have assumed that my brother, being older, could deal with Susie's death, and I guess it was also thought that, as young as I was, the event wouldn't have an impact on my life. Each of these assumptions demonstrates a fundamental misunderstanding about the capability of young children to understand events that are happening around them. At my mother's insistence, no one talked or reminisced about Susie, so why things had happened and were happening was never clarified. Nobody was ever asked how he or she felt about Susie's death. We were never asked if we wanted to talk about it. My mother's way of coping seemed to have been to pretend that Susie had never lived. If she had never lived, she could not have died.

My father must have been a brash young man. At sixteen, he was the youngest-ever graduate of the most academically elite of the city's public high schools and finished Wharton by the time he was nineteen. He graduated from the University of Pennsylvania Law School, played semipro basketball, and was heavily involved in local politics at the street level (which takes a particular kind of toughness)—first as a committeeman, then as a ward leader, getting out the votes for the Democratic machine. He rose through the ranks and eventually became the lawyer for the city's Democratic Party. This suggests a confidence and focus that no doubt enabled him also to successfully woo my mother, a noted local beauty. Ultimately, the party awarded my dad the judgeship he had coveted his entire professional life.

My father had a keen intellect; his interests were diverse. As a lawyer in private practice, he argued and won the first case in Pennsylvania to hold that a man who had committed murder was not guilty by reason of insanity, and every year until that man passed, he sent our family a Christmas card. My dad loved history and language, was an avid golfer, gardener, and fisherman, and was an ardent Zionist. He played the piano regularly until, in old age, he couldn't read sheet music anymore. In my favorite photograph of him, he is sitting at the piano, glasses pushed all the way up on his forehead, squinting at the notes swimming before him. As both a judge and a lawyer, he was recognized for his honesty, humanity, and candor, and he was much beloved by many, a mentor to countless up-and-coming attorneys.

I would not describe his relationship with me in the same way. Perhaps he embraced the opportunity to nurture those who were not his children because he was unable to understand his own. After Susie died, my father's need to be in control seemed to have, understandably, increased. He judged me, and I did not satisfy his standards. From my perspective, he was aloof and often seemed angry and unapproachable. Afraid of incurring his wrath and his disappointment, I kept secrets from him, and keeping secrets created walls. Did I remind my father of his ultimate powerlessness to control what mattered? Did I remind him every day of Susie?

After my dad was diagnosed with cancer, he used the time he had left to take everyone who mattered to him out to lunch or to dinner. The last thing he did before he died was his taxes. The morning he died, I went into the bedroom where he lay and sat next to him. I looked at him. I had no real sense of the man who lay in front of me. I had no sense of personal loss, that I had somehow been diminished. The body in front of me might as well have been that of a stranger. There was no connection; it was like the experience I had had when I examined the picture of my sister.

The lives of the dead set examples for us. It makes sense that having a sister die when I was only three left me afraid of a lot of things. It explains why the unexpected phone call is always bad news. It accounts for why, until I became a father, I was many times filled with an emotion I could articulate only as "the nameless dread."

An incident that is emblematic of my outlook at the time I became a father arose late one Wednesday morning. It was Yom Kippur, the Day of Atonement, the scariest day in Jewish theology, when God writes down what will happen to you in the next year based on your piety and observance of Jewish law. Jennifer and I had gone to services at a local university, and when they ended, we walked to our car only to find that we had received a parking ticket. That seemed a disastrous omen for what awaited us. I was shaken and angry.

Three days later, we got our stork call.

As one of my cousins described it, the boys literally, and on many levels, brought new life into the family.

When I became a father, I felt about as ready for the responsibility as would someone with a degree from a culinary school who has just been hauled on deck and told to steer a ship. As it turns out, the only way to learn how to be a father is to become one. I am grateful that my father inculcated certain core values that have proved to be beneficial guides, but I recall no open, candid conversations with him about serious personal issues. However, I can remember several moments when I learned how *not* to act—such as how damaging and counterproductive it is when a father loses his temper. My most disappointing moments as a father have been when I felt that I had acted too authoritarian and interjected anger into the moment. I would feel keen disappointment that I had become my father. His anger had driven me away; it had created a wedge between us. I desperately did not want my children to be afraid of me.

And certainly nothing that I have learned over the past thirty years of being a lawyer is of any use in being a father. One of the things drilled into new lawyers is never to ask a question to which you do not know the answer, because it could potentially damage your case. Of course, as a father you don't always have that luxury. Sometimes you *have* to ask questions you don't know the answer to, even if the answer might well be something you really would prefer not to hear.

When Noah and Dan were born, they were named by their birth parents, respectively, Thaddeus and Basil. (One of our friends suggested that they were given these names so that when they were adopted and given "normal" names, they would be eternally grateful.) One day in fifth grade, it was Noah's turn to be Star of the Week. Sooner or later, every kid in his class was given the opportunity to tell the others about his or her life: siblings, pets, what Mom and Dad were like, what their parents did for a living. So, Noah being Noah, I figured his birth story would be a part of what he told people. When I picked them up at school that day, after they had climbed into the backseat and gotten buckled in, I asked, "So how was your day, boys?"

"Great," Dan said immediately.

"Fine," said Noah curtly, almost dismissively, looking out the window. So I knew, or at least had a sense, that he was going through something. And then came the moment—the first time I had to ask a question when I had no idea what the answer or its ramifications would be. But I wasn't looking to prove a point or buttress an argument.

I asked, "Do you guys feel differently from your friends because you're adopted?"

"Not at all," said Dan.

"Yeah, sometimes I do," Noah said.

"Really?" I asked, looking at him in the rearview mirror. "How do you feel differently?"

"Well, sometimes I wonder what my life would have been like if we hadn't been adopted."

Dan immediately reached across the backseat and punched Noah in his left shoulder. "Well, for one thing," Dan said, "you'd have been Thaddeus and I'd have been Basil."

This cracked the ice as the moodiness dissolved in laughter.

Before I became a father, I relished my solitude. At the start of Labor Day weekend of the boys' senior year of high school, our plans to go to the Jersey shore to relax and shut down the house there were interrupted when an unexpected preschool project came up that required Noah to stay home. As Dan did not want to go without Noah, and Jennifer felt uncomfortable leaving them both alone, I went by myself.

My folks had bought the place back in the mid-1960s. It is a three-bedroom cottage, the smallest house on our end of the island and one of only two houses on the block that remain from the day they moved in. Since they had sold the house I grew up in thirty-five years ago, the shore house had become the repository of a lot of memories. I started spending time there as a junior in high school, and the summer freedom it represented had always been an integral part of my life.

Now I was uncomfortable being there alone.

oogy

Closing down the shore house always causes me to wonder about what will have happened in my life before we reopen it for the next summer. Seeing one of Oogy's chew toys in the living room made palpable the tenuous hold we have on what is dear to us. This was the start of the boys' final year at home, and image after image of them kaleidoscoped before me: running, laughing, standing on the rock jetty as the surf exploded around them, digging holes in the sand, making sand castles, cavorting in the surf with Jennifer. I remembered putting them in the car when they were toddlers and driving around so they would fall asleep. I saw them on the jetty as a storm rolled in, each wearing one of my hooded sweatshirts that reached to their ankles. I could see and hear them playing outside as they showered off the sand before coming into the house. I recalled my mom making us dinner, remembered putting them to sleep on the sofa bed, relived the smell of the clean sheets and the scent of their skin. I could see their sun blond hair, feel the heat of their bodies. They appeared before me, utterly exhausted, suspended in the sleep of the pure.

I had been part of an instrument of joy for them, and it made me feel complete. Laughter resounded within these walls, like distant thunder. It was still so odd for me to contemplate, after all that had happened in my life: How lucky was I?

CHAPTER 4 *Doors*

two months after the boys turned twelve, in January 2002, Buzzy, our black-and-white cat, began dying, an irreversible decline. It was like watching a slow-motion movie of a car crash without the power to alter the ending.

I had worked hard his entire life at keeping him alive. We had rescued Buzz when he was only five weeks old, and at the time no one thought he would survive. He had infections in both eyes and was so flea-ridden that we ended up having to hire an exterminator to bomb the house to get rid of the infestation. He weighed so little that we could have mailed him with a first-class stamp. He was not even the cat I had wanted. I had envisioned a white cat with black spots, and Buzz was the inverse of that. The first time I picked him up at the animal rescue, he climbed onto my shoulder and went to sleep, purring away as if he were being paid to be cute. To this day I do not know why, but I decided, He's not exactly what I want, but if he's here tomorrow, I'll take him. I came back to the shelter the next day, he was, and I did. He filled the house with his appreciation. He had been a loving friend, a boon companion, as they say. Buzzy never met a lap he did not like. The boys' great-aunts and -uncles would become electrified whenever Buzz jumped onto their laps, curled up, and started purring. He would ride around the house on my shoulder.

But now he was fourteen, and the end was facing us. When I came home from work one Friday, he was lying in his own waste underneath the dining room table. He had lost the power to move. A small hole opened in my heart. I cleaned him off with a warm, damp cloth and some pet shampoo. I wadded up a blanket from our bed that had our scent and placed Buzz on it in the dining room next to the radiator. Jennifer and the boys and I had made plans earlier in the week to go to a movie that evening, but about halfway through the film, I realized there was no way that I could stay. I was worried and sad and could not concentrate. I needed to be with Buzz; I was convinced that on some level, he would know I was there. I went home and sat next to him, reading a book while he slept. When the movie was over, I drove back and picked up Jennifer and the boys. We returned to the house; I put a pillow and blanket on the floor next to Buzz and curled up for the night.

I called Ardmore when they opened the next morning and told them I was bringing Buzzy over. The boys said they wanted to come to the hospital with me, knowing it was their last chance to say good-bye to the cat they had known all their lives. I was both surprised and moved by their willingness to confront sickness and death; it evidenced a remarkable strength and maturity. It was also a testament to their deep connection with him. I put the blanket in the cat carrier and placed Buzz inside. I put him on the passenger seat next to me while the boys clambered into the middle seats. I kept one finger touching him the entire ride. I wanted to reassure him. I thought if he could feel me stroking him, he wouldn't be afraid.

At the hospital, one of the technicians gently removed Buzz from the carrier and took him into the treatment room. Dr. Peters, one of the two doctors on duty, said that Dr. Bianco would give us a call Monday morning. And then, just as we were getting ready to leave, another one of the staff members emerged from the back of the hospital with a pure white pup on a leash. The dog was so eager to go for a walk that he was straining to get out the door, pawing at the floor. The dog was a visual oxymoron. The right side of him was adorable, but the left side of his face was all flamingo pink scar tissue; it looked as if it had melted. His head appeared swollen, distorted. His right ear was flopped over itself. His left ear was a jagged stump of flesh a thumb's width high. The back of his lower left lip drooped below his jawline. As soon as he saw us, he started this strange little dance. His head wagged one way and his butt the other; his tail whipped around as though he were trying to take off, which he was. His forepaws whirled on the floor as he tried to gain traction.

The dog strained toward us, and Noah went down on one knee. With a sudden explosive force, the pup tore the leash out of the technician's grasp and rocketed into Noah, knocking him over. Noah fell backward and lay stretched out as the dog stood on his chest, licking his face without pause. The boys started laughing as Dan reached over and began to pet the dog, who wriggled over to him and lapped at his face. I converged on the entanglement, and when I touched the pup, I felt that I had never met an animal with such soft fur. He was a plush toy come to life, as smooth as butter. I stood and cradled the dog in my arms as he licked my face and neck. The boys crowded around; the pup covered us with kisses. We fell instantly and completely in love with him. Seeing what was going on, the technician removed the leash from around the pup's neck.

The dog had run to us as though he had instantly recognized that we were his family and he had been waiting all of his life for us to arrive. He knew who we were to him. The union was instantaneous and complete.

I asked Dr. Peters, "What happened to him?" It seemed rather obvious to me that the dog had been badly burned in a fire.

Very matter-of-factly, as if he were telling me the score of a game, Dr. Peters stated, "He was a bait dog."

"What?" I asked. I was buying time to try to comprehend the enormity of his words. "What's a bait dog?" I had never heard that term before, yet I had a sense it was nothing pleasant.

"He was used as bait for a fighting dog. That's how they teach them to fight. They'll use anything they can get. Poodles, cats, you name it."

"Where do they get them?"

"Strays. Petnapping." He raised the first two fingers of each hand. "'Free to good home' ads. Wherever and however they can." He shrugged resignedly.

It was impossible for me to accept what had happened to this pup. To allow it to have happened under any circumstances—to have *caused* it to happen—was deplorable and repulsive. And there was something so radiantly special about this dog.

The pup had a muzzle that narrowed to a large black nose; his broad forehead, I later discovered, was the result of all the swelling from his injuries and the subsequent surgery. I thought he might be the kind of dog that General Patton had had.

"Is this a bull terrier?" I asked.

Dr. Peters laughed. "No, he's a pit bull."

"Where did he come from?" Dan asked.

"He was brought into the ER sometime over the weekend after a police raid. They found this guy bleeding to death in a cage. The SPCA told them to bring him here."

"Why here?"

"We're the only hospital around with an after-hours ER facility," Dr. Peters explained. "Otherwise, the hospitals on the Main Line get injured animals on a rotating basis."

"Do you know where this happened?"

"I don't. All I know is that Dr. Bianco operated on him for hours and managed to save him."

"Do you know how old he is?" Noah asked.

"Somewhere around four months. We can't really be sure."

"Of course," I said. "How long has he been here?"

"He came in in December, but I don't recall the date offhand. About a month."

By this time, I had put the dog back down on the floor, and Noah and Dan and I were kneeling and petting him. He was prancing back and forth among the three of us, licking away. But the assistant needed to get him outside to do his business, so we said good-bye and watched them head out the door for their constitutional.

"Who does he belong to?" I asked, certain that an animal with such charm and personality and with so much affection, and who had been at the hospital for several weeks, would by now have found an owner. I was hoping against hope that this might not be the case, and when Dr. Peters told me, "No one," I felt amazingly fortunate and gratified.

Then I said to the boys, grinning, "Guys? How about it? Should we adopt him?"

They both agreed without a moment's hesitation.

"Well," I said, "now that that's settled, we have to get approval from the CEO."

"Mom?" the boys asked in chorus.

"Sure. I'll call on Monday," I told Dr. Peters. "Don't let anyone else put in a claim for him until then, okay?"

"I promise," he said.

I felt giddy. I could not wait to get that dog into my house. When I took the boys back home, and we told Jennifer about the dog, she was less than enthusiastic. In fact, she said no.

She had her reasons. Our previous dog, also a rescue, had bitten a friend of the boys in an unprovoked attack; it had taken eleven stitches to close the gash in his face. Although that had happened over a year and a half ago, Jennifer was understandably fearful that an abused pit bull presented a realistic chance that someone, or someone's pet, might be brutalized. We asked her to come meet the dog and experience his personality, to talk to Dr. Bianco about it. To my surprise, she agreed. But she also said that she was going to ask Dr. Bianco if he could guarantee that the dog did not pose a threat, and if he gave her any response other than an unqualified no (which, she told me years later, she never thought he would be able to do), she would refuse to allow the dog in the house.

"This really is Mr. Happy Dog," Dr. Bianco told her the following Monday morning. "This little guy is one of the happiest dogs I have ever met." And then he added, smiling, "I can't imagine what he'd be like if half of his face hadn't been ripped off."

Dr. Bianco, Jennifer, and I were in one of the examination rooms with the pup, who lay on a steel table while Dr. B stroked his flanks. I was lazily rubbing his head, which he held erect, his dark eyes following us, his tail beating the table in a slow, steady rhythm. I reached down and touched his neck, began to massage behind his missing ear. The pup put his head down on the table while I stroked the softness just behind the scarring.

"We've already been through having a dog that bit someone," Jennifer said. "It was beyond horrible. A ten-year-old boy almost lost an eye and needed a number of stitches to close the wound."

"Luckily, his parents were remarkably cool about it," I said quickly, trying to steer this conversation in a more positive direction. I explained to Dr. Bianco that the boy's parents had accepted the incident as collective bad luck, since they understood we had rescued the dog just days before, and they had not initiated a lawsuit against us. They knew that we could not have known the dog was a biter. To this day, the boy has remained friends with Noah and Dan.

The rescue organization from which we had adopted that dog had told us he was a retriever/Airedale mix. We later learned he was mostly chow, and according to what we were told, the chow considers anyone besides his caretaker as fair game. We took the dog back to the shelter we had adopted it from the same day the boy was bitten. The shelter was a no-kill one, and we understood that eventually the dog went to live on a farm with an elderly woman who received few visitors.

"What I want to know is," Jennifer continued, "since this animal is an abused pit bull, how can we be sure that it'll never hurt anyone?"

Dr. Bianco looked into her eyes. "This dog doesn't have a mean bone in his body," he said matter-of-factly, without any hesitation. He shook his head. "He will never, ever bite anyone."

He is really going out on a limb for me, I thought. There's no way he can guarantee this, is there?

Based on Oogy's weight (thirty pounds), his size, and his breed, Dr. Bianco estimated his age at four months, confirming what Dr. Peters had told us.

"How big will he get to be?" I asked.

"Fifty to fifty-five pounds," he told us with a shrug.

Much to my surprise, Jennifer said she would agree to give it a try. Then she left for work.

I looked at the dog. I said, "You're coming home with us, pal." He cocked his head. His tail repeatedly whapped the steel table. It was clear that he understood something was going on. I gently rubbed the velvet in between his shoulders.

"Here's what we're going to do," Dr. Bianco explained. "We've already neutered him. He's up-to-date on all his shots. Diane has been taking him home to foster him. She has two little kids and half a dozen different animals in the house. We want to make certain he's safe around other animals and kids. Diane's also going to crate-train him for you and make sure he's house-broken. When she feels comfortable with his behavior, she'll give you a call and make arrangements to get him to you."

Then he added, "You've got yourself a great dog, Larry. The staff knows how much your family loves animals, and we're really glad you're taking him. We're excited for all of you."

"That's great," I told him. "Thank you very much." I rubbed the leathery texture of the scar tissue and the softness where the scar tissue ended. I had a sense that the opportunity to compensate for what had happened to this dog would somehow, in as yet indefinable ways, add to the experience. I looked forward to the opportunity to make the dog feel secure and appreciated. I experienced his immediate willingness to trust us with his well-being, after what he had been through, as a special gift.

I said, "We're the lucky ones, I think."

After leaving the hospital, I considered the uniqueness of the weekend's lessons. Facing the loss of a loved companion, we had started Saturday morning consumed by sadness, despondent, resigned to the unavoidable chasm that lay before us—and without any indication that anything other than bleakness would be our lot for the day, we had encountered a totally opposite experience. I knew the boys would appreciate the way in which events had unfolded. It represented a lesson one rarely had the opportunity to illustrate with such immediacy: life going out one door and in another. And then I started thinking about a name.

I laughed out loud. There was no way to deny it: This was one ugly dog. If his face had been a mask, no one would have wanted to wear it. Of course, I knew I could not call him that. I could not name a dog "Ugly." And then my thoughts jumped to a term I had used when I was a teenager—"oogly," as in, "Man, that is one oogly sweater." And suddenly, just like that, I said, "Oogy," out loud to myself and knew without a doubt that the pup had a name.

We mourned Buzzy for weeks, and to this day, I love to look at photos of him and the family. I remember Buzzy and the love he shared with tremendous fondness. But the gap in our lives was about to be filled in a sudden and decisive way.

CHAPTER 5 *The Arrival*

Over the next ten days, I prepared for the reintroduction of a dog into our lives. I went through the cupboards and drawers and found the water bowl and food bowl where I had stashed them. I found the retractable leash and the brush we had used for the dog we'd had before Oogy. I selected an old and very soft flannel blanket for him to sleep on in his cage.

I went to the grocery store and carefully considered the canned and dry dog food, perusing the lists of ingredients. I knew that a lot of dog food contained waste and chemicals and was of questionable quality. I examined the labels, trying to discern what would offer the most quality and nourishment. It was impossible to tell. I couldn't have known it at the time, of course, but finding

Oogy the right food would become an ongoing challenge that lasted years.

I also bought a green collar and a bone-shaped metal dog tag on which I inscribed "Oogy" and our home telephone number. I bought several different varieties of chews and treats to occupy him and to clean his teeth. I picked out some soft toys for him to tear apart. At home, I stashed these acquisitions in the kitchen's corner cupboard.

One evening a week later, Diane called and asked if I was going to be around the next morning. Oogy was ready for transitioning. She asked if we had come up with a name for him, and when I told her what it was, she laughed and commented that because it was two syllables, like "Eli," the name change should not prove to be a problem. There was a mild sense of excitement that evening; we were getting a new pet. None of us, of course, had any way of knowing that our lives were about to be changed in a fundamental fashion, just as much as if we had adopted another child.

That morning, after everyone was gone, I went outside and retrieved the newspaper from the curb near the mailbox. I sat on the couch in the family room, drank some more coffee, and read the newspaper all the way through. This was the only part of the day that was mine alone. I relished the quiet and the temporary lack of obligation.

When I was done with the newspaper, I put it aside for Jennifer to read that night, went upstairs and showered, then threw the laundry from the washer into the dryer and started that cycle. I was downstairs emptying the dishwasher when Diane's station wagon pulled into the driveway a little after nine.

I watched her exit and open the rear lift gate and take out several shopping bags, and went outside to help. She removed a folded-up black steel contraption, which was the crate in which Oogy was to sleep and which I took from her. Oogy, who was not Oogy yet but still Eli, placed his front paws on the top of the backseat and stared at me, his tail wagging furiously, and began to bark. I didn't know whether it was at me or at Diane. I carried the crate into the kitchen, and when I went back outside, I walked around to the back door of the car and opened it slowly. Oogy rushed forward like air escaping a vacuum seal, and I scooped him up, one arm supporting his butt; the other passed across his chest while I massaged his ear and the top of his head. He squirmed around until he was standing on his hind legs, the better to reach my face. He licked me unrelentingly.

Once inside the house, in the kitchen, I put him down

by his water bowl. Oogy sniffed it and then followed me over to where Diane was unpacking the shopping bags. He leaned against one of her legs and looked at me. I had a sense that he was appraising me.

Diane called him, fondly and interchangeably, "knuck-lehead" and "goofball." She said he was wonderful with her two kids and her pets, and that her dog would be relieved now that she was the only dog in the house again. Diane had housebroken Oogy (well, mostly, anyway, as we would learn) and crate-trained him as well. I had never used a crate before, but everyone I had ever talked about it with said that his or her dog felt safe within its steel bars and equated the crate with security. I had no reason to anticipate that Oogy's response to being con-fined would be any different.

The contents of the two shopping bags were a testa-ment to Diane's thoughtfulness and attention to what a young dog needed and what would occupy him and make him happy. She brought out several soft toys, flea and tick protection, heartworm pills, and a five-pound bag of dry food, explaining, "I'm not a big proponent of canned food. A lot of it is fatty junk." She told me to give Oogy the heartworm pills and apply the tick lotion every thirty days. We talked about how much food I should give him and how many times a day he should be fed. We dis-cussed how much exercise he would need. Diane told me that riding in a car seemed to upset Oogy's stomach. She presented me with some powdered medicine in case he developed diarrhea, as he had been prone to during his adjustment to real food. She took out and handed over a package of gauze pads and a blue antibiotic lotion that also served as a moisturizer and explained that I needed to wipe Oogy's scar tissue twice a day to minimize discomfort by keeping the scar tissue from drying out. Finally, Diane asked me where I wanted the crate set up. We walked down the hall, Oogy trotting along with us.

"I picked up some dog food as well," I told her. "Has Oogy eaten today?"

"I fed him before I brought him over," Diane told me. She asked where his new name had come from. I told her about my flash of inspiration.

The largest amount of open space was in the living room at the end of the hall. The only furniture in it was the baby grand piano my parents had given us, a coffee table between two small camelback sofas from Jennifer's mom, and my old stereo equipment and speakers. The turntable, tape deck, tuner, amp, and preamp had not been hooked up or plugged in since we had moved in nine years earlier, victims of technological advancements that had left them in the dust—literally and figuratively. In fact, I could not recall anyone ever sitting in that room other than me. Occasionally on a Sunday morning, I would do the crossword puzzle in there just to get away from the jabbering on the TV where the boys were in the family room.

Diane showed me how to unfold the crate and tighten the fasteners that held it into place. If I wanted to take it down and pack it, all I had to do was reverse the process. I took an old beach towel and spread it out on the floor, and we moved the box onto the towel to protect the floor and keep it from getting scratched up. I put Oogy's blanket in there and folded it carefully to provide maximum cushioning for him. I went back into the kitchen and found a plastic bowl from when the boys had been toddlers. Some long-forgotten form of superheros were cavorting inside. I put some water in it, and placed a section of newspaper under it in the box. Then Diane, Oogy, and I walked back into the kitchen.

"Thanks so much for everything, Diane," I said.

"I'm happy to be able to do it," she replied.

Just before Diane left, she knelt and gave Oogy a big hug and a kiss. When she stood, she rubbed her hands over the top of his head.

"I love this guy," she said. "He's an amazing dog, and because you're an animal person you'll understand and appreciate what this dog is all about. He is really very special. He and your family are perfect for each other. You'll have a great time, and your boys are going to have a best friend they'll never forget. In six months, we'll drop you a reminder to bring him in for a checkup." And then she was gone, and Oogy and I were by ourselves for the first time.

Somewhere outside, a truck beeped in reverse. Then the sound stopped, and it was still and quiet except for the humming of the dryer over my head.

I leaned against the dishwasher and looked down at Oogy. He stood, his head slightly tilted expectantly, his tail wagging. Did he have some sense that things would be different from now on? Having gone through what he had, and never having known anything else, what did he think was awaiting him?

"Hello, Oogy," I said. "From now on, that's you. You're Oogy. Oogy, Oogy, Oogy. Oogy for the rest of your days. Oogy ever after. You're in our family now," I explained. "There's me, I'm Dad; Jennifer, who is Mom; and Danny and Noah, who are twelve. You'll like the boys. They're lots of fun. They're in sixth grade and go to school up the street. We have a cat, Martha, who is upstairs at the moment. I'm not sure what she'll think of you, but we'll work something out. She's kind of old and set in her ways. Too bad you never got to meet Buzzy. He was the cat who died the weekend we met you. In fact, he's the reason we got to meet you. I think you and he could have been pals." My back against the dishwasher, I slid to the floor and started to pet him gently. He began to lick my hands and arms, then started on my face until I pulled back. "We're going to take good care of you," I told him. "You won't ever have to worry about anything again. You won't ever have to be afraid of anything again. You will never be hungry or scared again. That's my personal promise to you. Will you trust me on that?"

Oogy did not answer me. He did not acknowledge what I had said in any way. But his chocolate brown eyes seemed to be taking me in.

"High-five?" I asked.

I gave him a moment to comply, and when it became apparent that he would not, I said, "Okay, then. Here's what we'll get started with."

I stood back up. I took his new collar, picked up the ID tag I had purchased and the rabies tag Diane had brought along, and then reached into the tool drawer and pulled out needle-nose pliers. I pried open the steel piece on the collar, slid on the tags, and closed the steel back over them, securing the tags into place. Finally, I sat back down, reached over, and lifted Oogy into my lap.

"This makes it official," I said. I kissed his nose, and he licked me. "You now have your name and our phone number. So now there's no excuse for not calling if you run off or get lost."

I crossed my ankles in front of me and settled Oogy

onto my lap. Experimentally, I placed the collar around his neck and clicked its plastic prongs into place. The collar was a tad large, so I removed it, tightened it up, and snapped it into place again. I took comfort in the fact that Oogy was now identified with our telephone number, confirmation that he belonged with us.

I placed him back on the floor and stood up again. I tore open the end of the package that held the gauze pads and pulled one out, then cut the pad in half with a pair of scissors. Oogy backed up a few steps, but his gaze never left me. I opened the bottle of blue lotion and spread some onto the gauze. Then I sat back down on the terra-cotta-tiled floor of the kitchen, which was cool beneath me, and patted my lap.

"Come here, pal," I said. "Come over here."

Oogy looked at me.

"Come here, my friend." I patted my lap again.

Oogy looked at me.

Holding the moistened gauze pad in my right hand, I craned my torso, reached over, and gently picked him up. He did not resist. I felt the warmth of his flesh and the smoothness of him and the tensile strength of his rib cage. Depraved acts had been committed against him, yet he sat before me waiting for my love and help.

I said to him, "No bad thing will ever happen to you again."

I placed him between my legs, and he sat with his back to me. I ran my hands over both sides of his head, careful not to draw any distinction between the scored and the intact parts of his face, and then stroked down the sides of his body, the flanks of his rear legs. I reached underneath and scratched his belly. I slowly scratched behind his remaining ear. And then, for the first time, just as I would every morning and evening for the next six months, I began with small, circular strokes to rub the dampened gauze pad over the raw pink flesh that was the left side of Oogy's head. It was as though I were trying to wipe away what had happened to him. The blue liquid turned soapy-looking as I massaged the leathery skin. I talked quietly to him the entire time. "Yes," I told him, just as I would tell him every time, "you're a *good* boy. This didn't happen because of you. This does not mean that you are a bad doggy, an undeserving dog. We love you very much. You didn't deserve this. Nobody does. This has nothing to do with who you are. You're a lovely doggy. You'll never have to be scared again. No one and nothing will ever hurt you again."

I think that the first thing I did with Oogy, acting to assuage his wound, initiating immediate and intimate contact with the symbol of his vulnerability, helped to set the tone for all that was to follow. I took pleasure in the intimacy of this act, in my ability to nurture and support the precious vulnerability of this amazing little being. I felt privileged to be able to do it. Oogy never moved or fidgeted or tried to pull away.

When we were done, I rose and threw the gauze into the trash. I consolidated all the chew toys in a cookie jar and all the soft toys and rubber toys in a wicker basket in the family room. Oogy followed me back and forth as I did this. I put his medicine on a different shelf in the same cabinet where our own medicines were stored. Afterward, I poured myself a cup of cold coffee and nuked it in the microwave for fifty seconds. I said, "Follow me, my friend," as though anything else were even remotely possible. With Oogy alongside me, wagging his tail as he sauntered along, I walked back down the hallway into the family room, where I had been sitting alone an hour before. I sat on the couch and said, "Here ya go, pal," and patted the seat beside me. Oogy climbed up and sat there, leaning against me while I cupped his ear and rubbed his neck. Then he rose, circled several times, curled up against me, lay down with a snort, and went to sleep. Mornings were no longer mine alone, and I was thrilled about it.

I slowly drank the coffee and simply luxuriated in the experience of having this dog's warmth planted against my thigh. Then I stood and headed for the kitchen. Oogy immediately jumped off the couch and followed me. I placed the cup in the sink and picked up the leash off the table. Kneeling, I attached the clip on the leash to Oogy's collar. I put on my old red-and-black wool mackinaw, opened the back door, and walked with him out into the yard. I let the line play out about ten feet and locked it. Oogy meandered here and there, all new smells for him to assimilate and define. We did two full tours and then returned to the house. I removed the leash and went upstairs. Oogy followed me.

We walked into the bedroom. Martha was plumped up in the middle of the bed, as if in meditation. She did not even look at Oogy. When he saw her, he barked. It wasn't an angry bark. It was a short one, intended to make certain that she knew he was around and to get her attention. Nothing changed in her demeanor. He barked again. As I was to learn, animals that didn't want to play with Oogy frustrated him.

"Forget about it," I told him.

Martha lived another two years, and from the day that Oogy walked into the house, she never left our bedroom again. Oogy would occasionally come up to the bedroom, where she sat serenely on the bed, and would bark and bark at her, but she paid him no attention whatsoever. She wouldn't even deign to turn her head and look at him. He never would have hurt her—Oogy had slept next to an eighteen-year-old cat on the floor of the reception area every night when he had lived at the animal hospital. It was not that Martha was afraid. She was simply not interested—a *grande doyenne* with no time for the riffraff.

Oogy and I passed through the bedroom into the laundry room as he sniffed at everything, getting his bearings, starting to learn the parameters of his new world. I wondered if any of the smells he was absorbing encouraged him by reminding him of his ecstatic initial reaction to Noah and Dan. After I'd changed out of my sweats, we went downstairs, where I put on my sneakers. Then it was time for me to leave. I walked Oogy into the living room and opened the door of the crate.

"C'mon, Oogy," I said, expecting he would rush in. Crate-trained dogs just loved being in them, right?

Oogy turned and walked into the hall, where he lay down in the doorway, put his muzzle on his forepaws, and looked at me dolefully. His back legs were splayed out like those of a frog. He could not have gotten any closer to the floor unless he had been glued onto it. I called him again, but he did not budge. I patted the side of the cage, as though the sound would entice him or remind him what this was really all about. He did not move. I walked over to him. I bent at the waist and patted my knees.

"I need to go to work," I said. I was surprised by his reaction. Oogy clearly had zero interest in going into that crate.

"C'mon, Oogy. You need to get into the box."

Oogy did not move.

I went back to the crate and called his name several times without, it seemed to me, the slightest hint of threat in my tone of voice. Oogy continued to lie on the floor and stare at me.

As he was not going to cooperate, my only solution was to pick him up and put him in the crate, which I did. He struggled and resisted. I had to push his behind in and swiftly shut the door, sliding the latching mechanism into place. As soon as he was inside, he turned around and began barking furiously. Each bark was as loud and as distinct as a gunshot in a train car.

Separation anxiety, I told myself.

"I'll be back, you don't have to worry about that," I said to him. "I won't leave you alone for more than a few hours. I want to be here when the boys get home."

Oogy continued barking. He barked as I left the room and walked down the hall, and when I went into the driveway I could hear him barking and barking. I felt terrible that he missed me so much and thought he had been abandoned, but I saw no other choice. I needed to go to work, and I had to believe, based on what everyone had told me about crating, that Oogy would adapt and feel protected within its confines.

I knew the boys usually got home from school at a

little before three, so I made sure to beat them by fifteen minutes. When I opened the back door, Oogy immediately began barking, and I could hear him banging around in the cage, his tail whacking the sides, making the metal joints ring like some atonal wind chime. His complete and utter joy at seeing me walk into the living room warmed my heart. I knelt and opened the door of the cage and he burst out, running around and into me while I patted his head and flanks and rubbed his back. That excitement level continued unabated as we walked back into the kitchen, where I put him on the leash and took him outside. As we were completing the second circuit of the house, I saw the boys crossing the neighbor's front yard. When they saw Oogy, they came running over, surrounding him. They dropped their backpacks and knelt, and he raced back and forth between the two of them. I thought back to the laundry room earlier in the day and our first meeting and wondered what connections might be reverberating in his head.

"Welcome home, Oogy," Noah said. "Welcome to our house."

"We're glad you're here," said Dan. "You're part of our family now."

The four of us went into the house. In the kitchen, the boys shed sweatshirts and backpacks. Oogy followed them into the family room, where the boys sat on the couch.

Oogy jumped up and sat between them. He was already a part of them, and they each placed a hand on him. I sat on the coffee table in front of them and told them everything Diane had told me. I explained about the crate, the blue lotion, what behavior to expect. I told them it would be nice if they participated in walking and feeding Oogy. While experience told me there was little chance of that happening, it was worth a shot. But to see the way the three of them now sat together on the couch was the most important thing. Really, it was the only thing.

The boys' late afternoon routine consisted of snacks and some TV to decompress. Oogy whined and barked at them while they ate, demanding to be included. Later, the boys began their homework while I started dinner and, afterward, did the dishes. When they tried to do their homework at the same time, Oogy refused to let them. He yapped and ran around, bit at their cuffs, picked up a chew toy, and butted them with it. As soon as someone paid attention to him, he calmed down. As a result, the boys quickly learned that one of them had to keep Oogy company, pay attention to *him*, while the other worked. After I was done cleaning up, I took over keeping Oogy occupied, giving him the attention he craved. He insisted on recognition. He insisted on inclusion. The family dynamics had been completely altered.

Jennifer had called to say she was going out to dinner

with a client and anticipated she would be home sometime around 10:00. She asked how Oogy was doing.

"He's great," I told her. "The boys are madly in love
with him already."

After giving Oogy a peanut-butter bone, which I
placed on an old blanket that forever after would be
Oogy's dedicated bone blanket, I sat on the couch and
read. When he was finished with his bone, Oogy climbed
up next to me and went to sleep. I realized that once
Oogy understood that he could get my attention, his
need for it changed.

After the boys had completed their homework, they
joined us on the couch.

That night, Dan took his bath first. I filled the tub for
him, testing the water, which he never liked to be too
hot. Oogy stood in the room with me while I did this,
then followed me downstairs while the tub filled and
went back upstairs with Dan and me for the bath. I left
the two of them in the bathroom, the door open, while I
folded laundry.

Suddenly Oogy began barking, the sound reverberating off the walls of the bathroom like a dinner bell. I
turned my head to look from where I was seated on the
floor by the mound of clean laundry that always seemed
to overflow the basket. Dan was submerged, completely
out of sight, rinsing off his hair. Oogy had placed his

forelegs on the side of the tub and raised himself in alert; the boy he loved had disappeared. As soon as Dan brought his head out of the water, Oogy's anxiety disappeared and the barking ceased. Dan then moved closer to Oogy through the softly lapping water with an almost instinctual understanding of what would calm him. Oogy began to lick Dan's face.

I helped Dan towel off, relishing the fruity scent of the shampoo, after which I drained and refilled the tub for Noah. Oogy stayed downstairs with Dan while Noah bathed. Then we were ready for the next phase of Oogy's introduction into our lives.

From the first day that the boys had come home, we had read to them after bath time, a routine we followed, and which deeply involved us, until the boys started high school. It was a wonderfully bonding experience. Jennifer and I would take turns reading to them if we were both at home when bedtime arrived. Otherwise, whoever was at home would do it.

The boys had slept in the same room until they were ten. They were in cribs side by side for their first three years, and one would invariably climb over the sides into the other's crib, and they would giggle and cavort until they fell asleep next to each other. After we moved, they slept in bunk beds and, for years, still often slept together. After the bunk beds, too, had been outgrown, as part of the process of confirming their separate identities, each of the boys got his own room, and each got to pick the color of his room. We alternated the room in which we read each night. Depending on how tired they were, the boys would still frequently fall asleep in the same bed.

The first night Oogy was with us, I read to them in Noah's room.

I put a pillow against the wall and stretched out lengthwise across the foot of the bed. The only light came from a lamp on the windowsill to my right. The boys climbed in and got under the covers, their feet facing my left side. Each was wearing one of my T-shirts to sleep in, as they did every night. Oogy jumped onto the bed and curled up at their feet between them. I read for twenty minutes, and by then Noah was asleep, as was Oogy. I asked Dan if he wanted to go to his room.

"Stay here," he mumbled, his eyes unable to open. Then he turned on his side and drifted off.

The original plan had called for Oogy to spend nights in the sheltering confines of his crate. But when the time came, I simply could not bring myself to remove him forcibly from Noah's bed to put him in it. I thought of his insistent barking earlier in the day when he was separated from human contact, and since he would not be alone and I couldn't imagine him leaving the bed for anything, let alone to destroy the house, I decided to give Oogy the benefit of the doubt. Clearly, he was much happier here than he would be alone in his crate. And after all, wasn't this what it was all supposed to be about, anyway? What would be served by separating Oogy and the boys when they could stay together like this? He had slipped into place without disruption. It was almost as though he had always been there.

I reached over and switched off the lamp. The picture of the three of them sleeping together that first night, illuminated by light outside the window, where a strong wind rustled the trees, imprinted itself indelibly in my memory. Two young boys, backs to each other, curling hair against the pillows, and a little, white one-eared dog between them. Then, exhausted by the whirlwind events of the day, the book on my lap, I drifted off, and the four of us slept, me at a right angle to the three of them, until Jennifer came home and woke me.

"Hello, Oogy," she whispered sweetly. "Welcome to our house."

His tail thumped the bed, but otherwise he did not move. He was surrounded by love for the first time in his life, and he was not about to give that up for anything.

Years later, Noah told me that he remembered lying on the bed with Oogy that first night, and he thought, I hope my parents felt as good about us the day they brought us home as I feel about this dog right now. Oogy's need for contact, the way he leapt onto the bed with them as though he were perfectly entitled to do so and went to sleep between them, allowed Dan to immediately appreciate that there was something special in the nature of the dog.

The fact that a brutalized, mutilated pup had so immediately and so completely reposed his trust in us made all of us feel that we had been rewarded.

He was one of us.

CHAPTER **6** *The Third Twin*

he next morning, the second day of Oogy in our lives, when the alarm went off and I managed to wrestle myself out of bed, I did not make it three feet before I heard a thump from Noah's room, the clacking of toenails on the hardwood floor, and the jingling of the tags on Oogy's collar as he ran to greet me. I dropped to one knee and said, "Good morning, pal. Good morning, Oogy. Did you sleep okay?" I gave him a vigorous rubdown, slapped him gently on the flanks. "And what would you like for breakfast this morning?" I asked him. "Pancakes okay with you?"

He followed me into the bathroom, standing there while I washed my face and brushed my teeth. He followed me downstairs into the kitchen, wagging his tail the entire time as though it were motorized. I mixed up his food, and snuffling and grunting, he bent to it. After starting the coffee, I clipped the leash on him and we headed outside, where a bitter wind was blowing. His fur was so short that I wondered if I should buy him a protective covering of some sort.

When we went back inside and I planted myself at the foot of the stairs to call upstairs to wake everyone, Oogy was by my side. In the kitchen, while I made breakfast for the boys, Oogy lay on the floor watching me. He sat with the boys while they ate, wandered upstairs with them while they dressed, sat with them while they watched TV, joined us in the kitchen when they left for school. From the moment he had crossed the doorsill, he had been inseparable from us.

And every weekday morning after Jennifer and the boys had left, and after we'd had our couch time and I was ready to leave the house, I would have to drag Oogy to the crate by his collar and push his backside into it, and he would bark and bark in protest. I wasn't insensitive to this, but I thought that since crate-trained dogs loved their crates, Oogy was simply complaining that we were leaving him alone and that once he was alone, he would surrender to the safety the crate represented. It never occurred to me that something else might be going on.

Apart from his resistance to the crate, it was remarkable how thoroughly Oogy enjoyed whatever it was he encountered. He was so happy to be where he was that he almost seemed to be carrying an electric charge. When friends came to visit, as soon as he heard a vehicle in the driveway, Oogy would leap off the couch or whatever chair he was on and dash into the hall. For a moment or two his churning legs would search for a foothold on the throw rug there before he would go tearing out the back door. He would greet our visitors by placing both paws on whichever side of the car he could reach first, standing on his hind legs to peer in. As a young dog, he was also fond of standing up on his back legs and placing his front paws on the chest or shoulders of people he was meeting for the first time. This necessitated quite a number of red alerts around the elderly, including Noah and Dan's great-aunts and great-uncles. One afternoon, Jennifer was playing with Oogy in the yard when he started running in circles. I later learned this was an expression of sheer happiness. This time, though, after one of his circles had been completed, Oogy ran directly into Jennifer, knocking her down. Her right knee was swollen for days. We had no way of knowing at the time that the act of hurling himself against her was a reflection of what he had been bred to do.

Years before the boys were born, my brother had given me a cartoon he'd clipped out of a magazine in which a stern-faced judge in a black robe is looking down at a little doggy and, gavel raised, declares: "Not guilty, because puppies do these things." Diane had cautioned Jennifer that because Oogy was young and obviously so high-energy, his behavior might not always be what she would like it to be. She also told us that pups calm down after one and a half to two years. "It's almost like someone has thrown a switch," she said. While my overall approach was that nothing he did would shock or dismay me, it is fair to say that none of us could have possibly imagined the extent of the havoc he was able to wreak in his puppy days.

In his first six months with us, in addition to chewing up the futon couch, Oogy gnawed the middle out of the seat cushions of the two camelback sofas in the living room. He bit the eraser off any pencil he could find and would climb onto tables and desks to get at them. The decapitated pencils were left where they had fallen. He ate a pair of my glasses and a pair of my mother-in-law's glasses. He chewed apart a wooden drawer in the kitchen. He ruined videotapes, countless CDs and CD cases, pens, crayons, and markers. He broke through every screen on every door in the house and scratched the paint off doors when he wanted to get out. He ate the antennae off every landline telephone in the house and then ate them off the replacements. He ate boxes of crackers, cookies (packaged and homemade, it made no difference), and loaves of bread.

A number of Noah's and Dan's friends were afraid of Oogy's rapidly expanding size and strength; others were annoyed and even alarmed by the manic energy he exuded and that demanded constant attention. A few, or their parents, distrusted Oogy because of all the bad press pit bulls get. As a result, the number of the boys' friends who came to visit dwindled. When the visitor was someone Oogy did not know, he would get very excited. His favorite greeting activity was to bite guests at their ankles. As he became familiar with the visitor, his playfulness, or his sense of wanting to be the center of attention, would abate. Oogy quickly became as comfortable around the boys' friends as he was with the boys themselves. Those of their friends who continued to come by—all boys with dogs in their own households, as it turned out—quickly found themselves the object of Oogy's affection. After all, he could love Noah and Dan anytime and the rest of the time. It was not an unusual occurrence to come home and find Oogy draped over the lap of one of their friends while the boys sat on the floor playing a video game, or sleeping next to a boy sitting on one of the couches.

When Oogy came to live with us, for Noah and Dan it was in many ways like gaining a little brother. It soon became apparent to all of us that Oogy did not know he was not human; his bond with the boys made itself evident in incident after incident. Whatever the boys did, he insisted on being included; wherever they went, he wanted to go. When the boys ate, Oogy sat next to them watching them, barking at them for food as though they did not understand that he was right there and deserved some of whatever they were having. When the boys wrestled or had a pillow fight, Oogy threw himself into the mix. If they fought with each other, he would begin barking and jumping on them. When they played table tennis, he dashed back and forth with the ball, barking furiously, and when the ball hit the ground, there would be a mad, comic rush to see who got to it first; if it was Oogy, he would scoop it up, often without crushing it, just holding it in his mouth. If they were throwing around a lacrosse ball outside, he would race madly back and forth between them, following the flight of the ball and nipping at their ankles. When the three of us would throw a ball around, I was the only one whose ankles went unbitten. "That's because you're the alpha male," Noah suggested. If they went outside to have a catch or play basketball or football with friends, Oogy would demand to participate. If the boys left Oogy inside to go play football or to have a catch, he barked and whined incessantly and clawed at the door, alternately pacing back and forth, barking and yelping with frustration. Eventually, we realized that the only way the boys could play outside was for me to take Oogy off the property for a ride or a walk. We learned that if Oogy saw them leave the house before he did, he would try to follow them and would be uncooperative about getting into the car. As a result, when they wanted to do something outside, I would ask how much time they needed and would head out with Oogy before the boys left the house.

Once the electronic fence had been installed, when the boys left the property Oogy would run their scent to the edge of the yard as soon as I let him outside and sit staring up the street after them. He would sit there as long as I let him.

Oogy simply had no idea that he was a being separate and apart from the boys. In his view, he shared his life with them, and therefore there was never a doubt that they shared their lives with him. Around our house, he became known as "the third twin." As with any little brother, Oogy's insistence on being with Noah and Dan and doing whatever it was they were doing could be annoying for them. I repeatedly had to explain to the boys that when they were home alone after school or home with friends, one of them had to pay attention to Oogy, because if they ignored him, he would most likely do something destructive.

"He's like a little kid," I told them.

"Yeah," observed Dan, "but one who'll never grow up."

One morning shortly after Oogy came to live with us, and before we had the electric fence, after the boys headed up the street to middle school, I went out the door with Oogy to take him for a walk. He immediately slipped the collar and took off after them, following their scent. I ran along after him, though in a moment he was gone from view. When I found Oogy on the playground, he was surrounded by a dozen kids, including the boys, and a teacher's aide. Oogy was sitting in front of the group. Several of the children were petting him calmly. I was somewhat embarrassed, but everyone else seemed to think that it was really cute how he had followed the boys up there. And I must admit, he had thoroughly surprised even me. I had run after him expecting the worst, some imagined manifestation of pit bull ferocity preprogrammed into my brain, when all there was to it was pure adoration of the boys and a desire to be with them.

From the outset, I was reluctant to discipline Oogy, as I was with the boys, by invoking anger, deprivation, or fear. Not only did I consider these techniques to be counterproductive, but I was worried that they might alienate him from us. And I especially didn't want to use them with Oogy. He had already spent more than enough time afraid. I didn't have it in me to do that to him again.

If there was a downside to this, I never saw it, but there were visitors to our house who found the extent of license Oogy enjoyed somewhat disconcerting. He sat and slept wherever he wanted, and on more than one occasion, he climbed onto the dinner table while we were eating. This happened one memorable time when college friends were over. They looked at Oogy as if he were on fire, and then back and forth at one another, and though they didn't say anything about it, I never heard from them again.

As he grew out of puppyhood, Oogy continued to have an appetite for mass destruction that would not abate for another year and a half. One morning when the boys were in seventh grade, he chewed a hole in Noah's math homework. Jennifer wrote a note to the teacher that began, "You're not going to believe this, but..." He tore apart insulated galoshes, flip-flops, scarves, sneakers, shoes, plastic fruit, and the head of one of Noah's lacrosse sticks. He chewed up hard rubber dustpans, fly swatters, and brushes. He ate books, barrettes, and toothbrushes, shredded newspapers, ripped apart magazines, and tore chunks out of books. There is a sizable glop of glue on the rug in the dining room because Oogy chewed the top off a bottle of the stuff, and there appears to be no solvent to dissolve it that won't also take the rug with it. I have no idea how he avoided doing major damage to himself with that one. He ripped open packages, tore apart mail, ate a whole tray of brownies, chewed into countless boxes of energy bars, and raided the trash relentlessly. He ate plastic figures of the Lone Ranger and Tonto that Dan gave Jennifer one year for her birthday.

One holiday season, a friend sent Oogy a package of doggy treats that she had made. The deliveryman put the package behind the front screen door and pulled up the porch mat so that passersby would not see it. The weight of the mat prevented Oogy from actually opening the screen door, but he was able to chew open the exposed corner of the box and clean out one whole container of treats. He also took a bite out of the card that accompanied the gifts; it showed a shamrock next to a cartoon image of a white dog with the words *Lucky Dog* on it. I photocopied that in color and sent the friend the copy so she would know how much Oogy appreciated her thoughtfulness.

Jennifer came home from her exercise and yoga classes one Saturday and found food strewn all over the floor in the kitchen, the refrigerator door wide open. She assumed that I had been cleaning out the refrigerator and had become distracted, and put everything back in place. When I came downstairs after showering, she asked me about it. I told her I had been doing no such thing. When this happened a second time a few days later, I finally realized what was going on. I noticed that Oogy's bag of food was missing, as was some cheese and the lunch meat that had been in the cold drawer. The fruits and vegetables had not been touched. The beverages and salad dressings had not been opened. What was left of the missing bags of food was in pieces underneath the dining room table, which is where Oogy likes to take his illicit treasure. He seems to think of it as his little cave, where no one can see him.

Oogy had figured out how to open the refrigerator.

I put a bungee cord across the handles for the freezer

and the refrigerator adjacent to it. It was the only way to keep him out. On several occasions since then, though, when the last one of us to use the refrigerator has forgotten to clip the cord in place, Oogy has raided it. I can tell by his demeanor when I walk in the door. If he isn't there greeting me joyously but is skulking, his body low to the ground, head drooped but watching me, I know he is feeling guilty of something, and the first thing I check is the refrigerator. Then I go into the dining room and clean up the debris.

So far, the freezer has remained safe. However, there are two floor-to-ceiling storage cabinets Oogy started to open, randomly selecting boxes and bags of food to tear into. Each cabinet has two doors, so we also started to keep a rubber band wrapped around the door handles of each cabinet; another bungee cord prevented Oogy from accessing the trash; a third kept him out of the corner cupboard, where his dry food is stored. On more than one occasion, he has accessed each of these. He rarely will open any of these places when we are home and often will not eat what he has pilfered; it seems the sheer knavery of the act was important to him. He could also be counted on to take any food left on the counter at any time, and did so regularly.

It was never the loss of the food that bothered me, but the idea that he might ingest plastic to get at the food, which could lead to blockage and necessitate surgery. This is why I posted signs around the kitchen as well as on the back door reminding everyone to make sure the cords and rubber bands were in place when they left the kitchen or the house.

As he matured, Oogy's personality continued to exhibit a large portion of sheer mischievousness and playfulness. When I am making a bed, he will often jump onto it, lie down, and growl. He will roll onto his back, all four paws in the air, thrashing his head back and forth like a blind snake. He enjoys being covered with the sheet or blanket, wallowing around until his head emerges. Often when we are otherwise fully occupied, when I'm in the kitchen and the boys are doing homework, for instance, Oogy will pick up one of his soft toys and come into whatever room I am in and start bumping me in the butt with it. I am then supposed to stop whatever I am doing and follow him into the dining room, get down on all fours, and plod after him, chasing him under the table and around the chairs, while wherever he is, he will move someplace else under the table and growl at me while I veer in that direction. I have to let him win the tug-of-war that ensues when I am finally able to grab what he has in his mouth. Eventually, he will stop chewing on the toy and luxuriate in the attention I give him, which, after all, is what he has been after from the outset.

Almost every evening before settling down to sleep, he cases the room where the boys are watching TV or working on their laptops. He will go to the windowsills, the TV stand, the bookcase, the coffee table, until he finds something he knows he is not supposed to have, and he will grab it: a wallet, a flip-flop, a DVD box, a baseball cap. When we take it from him, he will go after something else. This last spasm of energy is a routine part of his day. When he has gotten over whatever it is that drove him to look for trouble, he will curl up next to one of the boys and sleep until morning.

To this day, if somebody cannot find something, Jennifer will suggest taking the search outside to see if Oogy has been working on it. The case for her cell phone has teeth marks in it. So do my favorite baseball cap and my new loafers. There is a picture of Dan and Oogy in the family room in an aluminum frame that has Oogy bite marks on it in the top left corner. I could not have thought that up, but it is not a bad marketing idea: customized frames with bite marks on them for people to use for pictures of their dogs. Oogy holds the copyright.

Eventually, as Diane had promised us, for the most part Oogy's destructive forays ceased. There would always be the purloined piece of cheese, the gravy-smeared foil under the dining room table, but, as though exorcised, whatever it had been that drove him to his small frenzies disappeared as Oogy matured, and there came a time when we no longer had to worry what awaited us each time we returned home.

But we still use the bungee cords on the refrigerator.

CHAPTER 7 *Surprises*

Since it would be good for Oogy's health to be able to run around in the yard and would keep him from chasing after people in the street, we decided to have a new electronic fence installed. The one in place when we had moved in had long since corroded into dust. The first company I called asked me what Oogy's breed was. When I told the agent with whom I was dealing that Oogy was a pit bull, she told me that her company would not install an electronic fence. It was their policy; they were afraid that if a pit bull got through one of their fences and attacked someone, they might be sued. The second company I called said that his breed would not be a problem.

An electronic fence is set up by inserting wire around the perimeter of the property, which is then marked by a series of small plastic flags. A charge runs along the wire controlled by a box attached to the house. Two conductive electrodes in a special collar rest against the dog's neck. If he gets too close to the fence, he will hear a buzzing sound intended to warn him away; if he continues, he will receive a shock. I had to know what the experience felt like, so I held the collar in my hand and walked to the fence. It was as though I had stuck my finger into a live lamp socket.

Once the fence had been installed, it was time to train Oogy. I was shown how to lead him up to it until he heard the buzzing sound, the warning that he was approaching the perimeter. The first time we did this, Oogy did not know that there was any significance to the sound, and I had to let him get shocked. The idea was that he would associate the warning sound with getting a jolt of electricity. After that first experience, I repeatedly led Oogy up toward the fence until he heard the cautionary sound, then immediately pulled him back and away from the fence line so that he learned to associate the sound with the limits of his domain.

However, I encountered an unexpected problem with training Oogy. Because he has only one ear, he cannot triangulate sound. As a result, he appeared to be confused about where the warning sound was coming from. It seemed likely to me that because he could not tell where the sound was coming from, it might not act as a deterrent for him; that he might go forward when he heard the warning sound, not back away. Since I did not want to subject him to repeated shocks, I called the company that had installed the fence and explained my concern. They sent over a technician who assessed the situation and suggested that I sight-train Oogy. I would pull him up close to the fence line and wave one of the little blue flags when the warning sounded and then pull him back. As smart as he was, Oogy made the connection and visually learned the limits of the yard in short order.

I was warned that any dog was likely to go through the fence once and that once was usually enough to convince the dog not to repeat the experience. One day, not long after the fence had been installed and Oogy had been successfully trained, Noah and Dan were throwing around a lacrosse ball in the street. Oogy, of course, was having trouble with that arrangement. He was dashing back and forth on the lawn and barking. I could hear him, but I was not paying much attention. Suddenly, Dan was at the back door calling for me, and I was aware that the barking had stopped.

Oogy had gone through the fence to be with the boys.

He was sitting in the street, shivering, utterly stunned. He looked as if he had run into the side of a truck. I had to drive the car into the street to pick him up because he would not come back the way he had gone out. To this day, I have to drive him through the fence line whenever I want to take him for a walk. If I am carrying the collar in my hand and I get too close to the fence, when the buzzing sound starts, Oogy retreats.

Outside of the house, we regularly encountered negative reactions from people simply because Oogy was a pit bull who had evidently been involved in some sort of fighting adventure. These reactions were not based on the facts but clearly reflected prejudices based on all the negative things written about the breed. It was not unusual for people we encountered on walks to step out into the street so as not to have to get too close to him. Any number of times I tried to reassure them that he was very friendly, but his looks seemed to confirm their mental associations and frightened them.

On one walk that first spring, we passed by a party in progress at a neighbor's house. A little boy was standing on the sidewalk with his dad. When Oogy started over to say hello, the dad asked, "Is that a pit bull?" When I answered that he was, the father very slowly picked up his son and walked backward into the house, keeping his eyes on us when he was not glancing back over his shoulder to see where he was going, and closed the door.

Another time, an elderly female neighbor had just exited her car as Oogy and I ambled by on one of our regular strolls. She asked, "What happened to your dog?"

I told her that he had been used as bait for a fighting dog. "I hate pit bulls!" she said dismissively. And I was thinking, But you're looking at one...

I still remember the look of revulsion and fear in the eyes of a woman we encountered at a local shopping center. Oogy and I had turned the corner from the parking lot to the sidewalk leading past a row of shops, and as soon as this woman saw us her eyes widened, she put both arms around her little boy and, before he knew what was happening, had dragged him inside the swinging doors of a store. Then, arms still around her son, she watched us through the glass facade as we passed. I gave her a big, friendly grin as we did so.

Not long after we had adopted Oogy, while I was taking him for a walk, we encountered two well-coiffed poodles with the total antithesis of Oogy's tough-guy looks, and they started yapping at him. They sounded like Oogy on helium. When a dog barks at Oogy, he invariably looks at it as though it is a creature from another dimension. The only time Oogy will bark at a dog is if he cannot get to it to play, such as when we're in the car and pass another dog walking by, or if he wants to play but the dog is ignoring him. I went to pull him away, but he slipped out of his collar and ran up to the poodles. Their owner panicked. While the only real danger that these poodles were in was that Oogy might accidentally step on one of them, this woman reacted as if her dogs were about to be tossed into a wood chipper. Her alarm, compounded by the yelping of her dogs, fed on itself and grew until I managed to grab Oogy, slip his collar back on, and drag him away.

The next day, a different neighbor passed me in the street. "I hear your dog went after the poodles," she said.

That was the owner's story, and she was sticking to it.

Walking with Oogy in the early days was like strolling with a mayoral candidate. He wanted to meet everyone he saw on the street. He would pull me like a small tractor to go over to the person, and if I would not cooperate, he would lie down in the street and refuse to go anywhere until the object of his attention had disappeared or, as usually happened, I relented and allowed him to go meet the person.

As the months passed, people from the neighborhood who were afraid of Oogy always changed their minds about him once they actually got to meet him and experienced his gentle, affectionate nature. It was not that people's fear of Oogy was illogical or unreasonable. His face was frightening, and none of these people had any way of knowing that his barking was not designed to scare them. On the contrary, he barked and paced to tell them he was frustrated because he could not meet them. Unfortunately, none of these people were conversant in Dog.

One evening several months after Oogy had joined

our family, he and I were out for a stroll when we saw a young woman approaching us. She was power-walking and talking into a headset at the same time. As she drew closer, I heard her say, "Ma, here's the dog I told you about, the one I'm afraid of?" I stopped. Oogy stood and looked at her. His tail wagged slowly back and forth. She approached us cautiously.

I said to the woman as she drew nearer, "It's okay. He's perfectly safe. I wouldn't be keeping him here in front of you if that wasn't the case."

After a brief hesitation, the woman came over to Oogy. She held out one hand, and he sniffed it. Then he licked her.

"I am so afraid of your dog," she said, "that I stopped jogging by your house."

"There's absolutely nothing to be afraid of," I assured her. "He only barks at you because he wants contact with you."

"He seems very nice," she admitted, nodding.

"He's more than very nice," I told her.

She cupped her hand under Oogy's muzzle. Then she knelt and, fascinated by the texture of his fur, began to stroke his head and shoulders. Oogy lifted his head and licked her face. She asked me what had happened to him, and I told her. By the time the encounter was over, the woman was kissing Oogy on the top of his head and massaging the muscles in his neck while he backed into her in appreciation.

Similar encounters happened on several occasions, and people's hesitancy if not fear dissolved once they actually met Oogy.

There have also been times when we have been able to use Oogy's intimidating appearance and apparently aggressive behavior to our advantage. Whenever there were strangers working in the neighborhood, I made it a point to let Oogy out of the house. "If someone is thinking of coming into our house," I assured the boys when they were younger, "once they take a look at Oogy and hear him barking, they're going to start thinking about looking for another house." Once Oogy had joined the family, the boys lost any lingering sense of discomfort they might have had about being alone.

While, thankfully, I've never had occasion to test this theory, I have always felt that if Oogy sensed we were afraid or if he perceived some threat, he would immediately transform himself into a completely different animal from the one we have encountered in his life so far. Out and about or in the house, in the blackest of the night, I have never had any fear that someone will physically threaten us or do us harm. In my heart, there has been no doubt that the dog we adore and who kisses us incessantly could and would react instantly to protect us at all costs—that he would die for us rather than let us feel threatened or allow us to be hurt. Oogy is a guardian who, I am convinced, will do whatever needs to be done to save us from peril.

One summer day, we came into the house and discovered that a window and screen were wide open in the family room. Nothing had been taken or moved. None of us would have had any reason to open the screen, but just to make sure, I asked the boys if they had done it. They told me that they had not, and we concluded that someone had decided to force his way into the house through the window, had heard and/or seen Oogy, and within seconds had realized that he had had better ideas in his life. The sight of an eighty-five-pound dog with half a face barking and rushing to the window, the sound of his growling reverberating in the room, had to have been a sobering experience.

True to Diane's word, six months after we had welcomed Oogy into our home, we received notification from Ardmore that it was time for his first scheduled checkup. I made an appointment, and no sooner had I walked in the door with Oogy than Karen, the technician sitting at the front desk in the reception area, took a look at him and, after a sharp intake of breath, blurted out, "That's a Dogo!"

"What's a Dogo?" I asked.

Karen started to laugh. "I'm not sure," she said.

Not yet a year old and still growing, Oogy already weighed seventy pounds. He stood a little over two feet high at the shoulder and was about four feet from nose to tail. When he stretched out, the way he would to greet someone by placing his front paws on their shoulders, he was over five feet long. He had already far surpassed what we had been told his adult weight would be. The significance of this was that Oogy had to have been younger than the four months we were told he was when we adopted him. His estimated age at the time had been based upon his weight—thirty pounds—compared with what his weight was supposed to be when he was fully grown—fifty-five pounds. The fact that he was still growing, and that he was already twenty pounds heavier than the estimate given by Dr. Bianco for his weight as a grown dog, meant that he had to have been younger when we met him. Oogy may have been no more than two months old when used as bait.

When I look back at it now, I realize that Oogy's size should perhaps have tipped us off that he was not a pit bull; but it is hard to be objective and make a determination about a dog's breed based on a visual assessment of his size and weight when you have been told by someone who should know that the pup in your arms is a specific breed—especially when the actual breed is something that you, a dog lover, know nothing about. And, just as with a child, when you see a dog every day, the extent of his growth is so incremental that you can't fully grasp or appreciate the process or the end result. Besides, Oogy *looked* like a pit bull—or, more accurately, a pit bull on steroids.

At this first checkup, Dr. Bianco examined and ran standard tests on Oogy and pronounced him to be in perfect health. Oogy also had his toenails clipped (Dogos' toenails grow unusually quickly). The first few times the staff clipped Oogy's nails, they muzzled him; then Diane realized that if one technician stroked him while the other worked on him, there would be no problems. Dr. Bianco gave me drops for the itching in the gash that had been Oogy's left ear, which he pawed at constantly; it was repeatedly subject to yeast infections. Dr. Bianco recommended certain vitamin supplements, which Oogy has had every day since. Dr. Bianco also suggested an over-the-counter wetting solution for Oogy's left eye. Distorted by scar tissue, the eye could not fully close when Oogy slept, and as a result, it could not self-lubricate. Ever since then, Oogy and I have used the same eye lubricant, as I, too, have "dry eye" syndrome. Dr. Bianco then asked that we arrange to come back so that he could put a microchip in Oogy's neck. That way, if Oogy ever ran away and was picked up, he could be returned to us. Finally, Dr. Bianco told me to get rid of the retractable leash. Just the week before, he had had two clients whose dogs ran into the street before the locking mechanisms could be engaged, and both had been hit by cars. A dog as big and powerful as Oogy could easily present a similar problem, and he might even be able to break the restraint.

On the way home, I bought a different kind of leash.

After Dr. Bianco had concluded the examination, I went to the reception desk and took out my credit card, but Karen shook her head in the negative.

She said, "Oogy's a no-pay."

I asked, "What's a 'no-pay'?"

She explained, "That means you don't pay for any of Oogy's medical treatment here. Ever."

I was stunned. I had never asked for special treatment, and I certainly hadn't expected it. They had saved Oogy's life and entrusted that life to us. And in our separate ways, all of us have contributed to his welfare as best we can. In all the years that have passed since we adopted Oogy, Ardmore Animal Hospital has *never* charged a dime for anything they have done or provided for Oogy—and multiple surgeries, medicines, and checkups were all required at different periods throughout Oogy's life to maintain his health.

This speaks volumes both about the special nature of

the people at the hospital and about Oogy himself. Years later, Diane revealed that she had made the decision that day not to charge for Oogy's care. To begin with, she loved Oogy so much and thought his story so triumphant, she had been gratified that we also had immediately appreciated his special nature and had accepted him into our home without qualification and despite his horrific appearance. Then, when we brought him back and she saw how he was thriving in the environment we had created for him, she was thrilled for him and felt vindicated for all the effort that had gone into saving him. We were fulfilling the promise she had initiated, to cherish and care for this special animal. He *had* been worth it after all.

As soon as I got home that morning, I went online to research Dogos.

The breed is actually called Dogo Argentino. The first picture I saw of a Dogo looked exactly like Oogy. I stared at it in wonderment, looked away to Oogy sleeping on the floor beside me, then back at the picture on the screen. I began to scroll down the page. Because there is mastiff in the breed—the Dogo is also known as the Argentine mastiff—many of the other Dogos I saw in photographs had broader, rounder foreheads than Oogy's, but his appearance is generally typical.

The Dogo was developed in the 1920s to be a pack hunter and guardian who could be trusted with a family.

Dogos are bred to hunt puma (which damage livestock) and boar (which devastate crops), both of which were ravaging farms in Argentina because the farmers and landowners could not stop them or bring them under control. The Dogo is derived from a now extinct breed, the Dog of Cordoba, a fighting dog, and includes traits of the Great Dane (for size), boxer (liveliness and gentleness), Spanish mastiff (power), bulldog (ample chest and boldness), bull terrier (fearlessness), Great Pyrenees (white coat to deflect heat), pointer (sense of smell), Irish wolfhound (endurance and hunting instinct), and Dogue de Bordeaux (powerful jaws).

Adult Dogos typically weigh between one hundred and one hundred ten pounds. Because Oogy was mistreated in his first few months, however, he is comparatively small, weighing in at eighty-five pounds. Given Oogy's strength and power at eighty-five pounds, I can't imagine trying to take him for a walk if he weighed a hundred and ten.

A Dogo's temperament is a fascinating combination of ferocity and gentle devotion to his family. They are unrelenting and fearless hunters—and I do not mean a hunter like a pointer or a retriever, I mean a hunter as in a killing machine. The muscle structure of the Dogo is simply massive, and the breed has tremendous stamina. They can track their prey at a gallop over great distances and are capable of incredible bursts of speed. They are bred to corner and hold their quarry, but they are also capable of killing their prey if it attempts to attack them or break out.

At the same time, the breed is known for being extremely loyal and affectionate with their families and to crave attention from their owners. They are wonderfully tolerant of children. Protective, they will guard their territory against any intruder not welcomed by the family. In Argentina, there is a saying: "A Dogo does not sit at your feet, it sits on your feet." Conversely, the Dogo accepts without limitation people welcomed by the family. I learned that in addition to their valuable roles as hunting dogs, Dogos are often used for police and military work, in narcotics detection, for tracking, and in search and rescue. Dogos also make excellent guide dogs for the blind.

Dogos are not naturally aggressive with other dogs; aggressiveness was bred out of them, since they could not function as pack hunters if they were constantly trying to establish dominance. Oogy's lack of aggression has occasionally encouraged other dogs to attack him. He has been intentionally bloodied on half a dozen occasions by other dogs. Oogy will not tolerate another dog trying to assert dominance and will defend himself, but as soon as the other dog is pulled away, Oogy loses any interest in fighting. However, because of the Dogo's ferociousness in combat, they are routinely fought in South America, and the breed is one of four that has been outlawed in the United Kingdom. Some owners crop their ears because it makes the Dogo look more combative. Also, when a Dogo is hunting or fighting, cropped ears offer less of a target to the beast he has engaged. It is not simply coincidence that the dog that tore up Oogy ripped off one of his ears. A floppy or large ear is a target.

The Dogo is not commonly found in the United States. Few people I have met have even heard of the breed, let alone have been able to recognize one. I'm sure that a number of reasons would explain the "exotic" nature of the breed in this country, not least of which is the fact that a Dogo can typically cost thousands of dollars.

I once asked Dr. Bianco why he had thought Oogy was a pit bull. "Nobody ever sees Dogos here," he explained. "In all my years as a vet, I've only ever treated one other Dogo. So I was not thinking of the breed. It never entered my mind at the time that this dog might be a Dogo. He looked like just another pit bull to me."

When Oogy runs—actually, it is more like leaping than running—he thrusts himself forward in great bounds, all four legs in the air simultaneously like a greyhound. He can approach a top speed of almost thirty miles an hour—I once checked the speedometer to see how fast I was going as he raced alongside my car while he was still in the yard. His hind leg muscles are like coiled springs; they are so strong that when he sits and the muscles bunch, his butt does not touch the ground. He has a neck like a fireplug to protect him when he closes with his prey, with accordionlike folds of flesh bunched at the back of his head. A long rib cage curves back from a barrel chest to a whippetlike waist. Viewed from the front, Oogy's broad chest is shaped like a box, and from the side, his body shape appears rectangular in the chest, then narrows as it recedes to his rump. He has thin black eyebrows, fine white eyelashes, and eyes that appear bloodshot, part of his Great Dane heritage.

There are numerous black splotches under Oogy's short white fur, like those of a Dalmatian only much less pronounced, more like shadows of spots than spots. He looks as though a couple of paintbrushes had been shaken off all over him. One thing I really dreaded was telling Oogy that his career plans might not be as unlimited as he hoped. After reading about Dogos, I had to break the news to him that he could never be a show dog. "You've got too many spots," I told him. "From what I've read, to be a show Dogo you can't have more than one spot." I did not want him engaging in flights of fancy that he could never realize. I didn't want to encourage unrealistic goals in him. I thought he might take it hard, but he handled it with his usual aplomb.

A doctor who was present at Ardmore when I related this to him laughed and responded, "I don't think *that's* Oogy's big hurdle in terms of becoming a show dog."

When Oogy came to live with us, I assumed that with his short white fur there would be little shedding. I could not have been more wrong. There is Oogy hair over everything we own. In the cars, it looks like a dusting of some strange powder. Every week I have to rub him down with a hard rubber currycomb of the kind that is used for horses.

Reflecting the traits of his breed, Oogy loves hot weather. In the summer, he will lie in the driveway, soaking in the heat for hours at a time. When he comes inside afterward, he feels as warm to the touch as if he's been in a toaster oven. He enjoys the snow, but he hates the feel of rain on his skin and will not voluntarily go out in it. Sometimes I will drag him out into the yard in the rain, hoping he will do his business, but he will just trot around the house to get back inside as soon as he can. During extended rainy periods, it is not unusual for Oogy to leave us a gift, ordinarily in some out-of-the-way location such as the basement or up in the weight room.

Watching Oogy interact with other dogs is fascinating once you know something about his breeding. His bulk and speed, the way he thunders across the grass with his powerful strides, make me think of a Percheron or Clydesdale running among other horses—if he were any heavier, the ground would shake. There are faster dogs than Oogy, there are heavier and more graceful dogs, but none are more powerful. He is a marvel of genetic engineering. He is designed to run relentlessly, and that is what he loves to do. He does not go after sticks and he does not go after balls, and dogs that want to do nothing else frustrate him. He wants to run and he wants to wrestle. And when he is running with another dog or other dogs, he never takes the lead. He always runs alongside the lead dog, just at or behind his front shoulder, and sometimes he'll give the other dog a slight chest bump. He never tries to knock the other dog over, but something in his genetics compels him to make some contact. He will run until he is exhausted, collapse for a few minutes, and then be ready to run again.

Knowing the attributes of Oogy's breed went a long way toward helping us understand his behavior and the nuances that were expressive of his character.

We're used to coming home and finding Oogy asleep on the table in the kitchen or in the dining room. He likes to sit on the picnic tables at the dog park as well. I attribute that to the hunter in him. It seems logical that he would like to be up high to look for game. To give Oogy his due, there have been no jaguars or mountain lions in our yard since he came home with us. (Boars were never really much of a problem anyway.)

Oogy's hunting senses allow him to be aware of another animal long before I can see it, and often I never do. I have learned that when we are out at night and he stops in his tracks and peers into some bushes or down a dark driveway, if he stands there completely still and concentrating, his ear up, looking across a field, another creature is definitely there, although in all likelihood I will never know what it is. Sometimes he drops his head and stares, motionless, alerted to another presence out there, trying to determine what it is, as though he is more likely to sense it rather than see it, his whole being telling him something I cannot know.

During his first couple of years with us, whenever we were out for a stroll Oogy would try to go after every squirrel or rabbit that caught his eye. This behavior was so common that once, when someone asked me where his name came from, I replied, "It's Elvish for 'squirrel's bane.'" He never did catch anything. The breeding leaves him relentless, though. There are some chipmunks that live in the foundation of our patio. On a number of occasions, Oogy has stood out there and barked at them incessantly. Passersby would see a dog barking his fool head off at masonry. Oogy does not seem to care, no matter how many times I remind him that this behavior makes him look rather silly.

One of my favorite things to do, though I don't get to

do it nearly as much as I would like, is to stretch out on the couch, enjoying the luxury of free time, and have Oogy stretch out next to me. He will put his head in the crook of my arm or rest it on my shoulder, and I marvel every time at his regular and relaxed deep breathing. Just to feel the rhythmic beating of his heart is encouraging. I will routinely talk to him about different things. On more than one occasion, I have asked him what he would have been like if he had both ears. Would his personality or demeanor have been different? Would he love me just as much? Oogy will invariably look at me a moment, then turn his head away with the foolishness of the question, upon which he has so far refused to speculate.

"Do you talk to other Dogos?" I once asked him. "Can you somehow communicate telepathically? Is there a psychic Dogo connection because you are all so unique? If so, tell them you're loved. Tell them that it worked out okay for you. Tell them," I said, "that we love you like there's no tomorrow."

CHAPTER **8** *A Special One*

It has always been my belief that a pet owner has a special responsibility to do everything that can be done to make the pet's life as fulfilling and peaceful as possible. That responsibility is yours the moment you make the choice to take an animal into your life. Indeed, just as with children, once the choice to assume responsibility for another life has been made, it can be carried out only one way if it is to have any chance of producing maximum results: all the way. It's what Diane refers to as "above and beyond."

Since Oogy was rescued and his face was stitched back together, his life has not been simply a never-ending series of pleasant experiences. He has had four more major operations. None of them, separately or cumulatively, have adversely affected his nature and temperament in the slightest. If anything, with each ordeal his trust in us has increased. He knows that we will alleviate his pain. He knows that we will do the right thing for him. His faith in us calms him and calms us.

The first of the surgeries became necessary as Oogy grew and the scar tissue where his face had been continued to spread. The expansion pulled the left side of his face upward. One result of this was that he could not close his left eye completely when he slept; it wept constantly in an attempt to lubricate itself and regularly issued a green, mucuslike discharge we needed to wipe away. His upper lip was pulled back in a perpetual grimace, a sneer that exposed some of his upper teeth. Because of the distortion caused by the scarring and leathery, reptilian texture of the scar tissue, he looked almost like a *T. rex* on the left side of his face. We sometimes called him "dinosaur dog."

Once Oogy had come to live with us, it took no time at all for the scarring to become simply part of who he was; but seeing it through other people's eyes was unavoidable. Those who caught only a glimpse of Oogy often had a difficult time accepting what their eyes told them they were seeing. One side of Oogy's profile looked perfectly normal: a sweet, white dog face, a large, black nose, a floppy ear; the other side looked positively grotesque, with a nub of an ear, textured scar tissue instead of white fur, and an exposed upper canine. Often, people could do nothing more than stare at him in astonishment — and sometimes in horror — as we passed quickly away, leaving them to try to assimilate what they had just seen. Sometimes I would see the person who had caught sight of Oogy gesturing wildly to get the attention of others around him or her to have a look at "the creature" while we were still there.

And I would leave them behind, secure in the knowledge of the loveliness beside me.

But in addition to the deformities the scarring had caused, none of which should have presented any substantive health issues, it turned out that the spreading scar tissue had created a very real problem, one that I never would have detected on my own because of Oogy's ability to tolerate extraordinary levels of pain. When Oogy was about two years old and had stopped growing, during one of his routine checkups Dr. Bianco informed me that Oogy was in chronic pain because the scar tissue had deformed his facial muscles. He explained that given Oogy's genetic composition, he had not and would never have let on that he was suffering the kind of acute torment he was undergoing on an unrelenting basis. "Imagine that someone has grabbed you by your face and is pulling on it, twisting it out of shape," Dr. Bianco said, seizing the skin of his face just below his cheekbone and yanking it upward with both hands to illustrate.

"The pain may be bearable, but at best it is very, very uncomfortable."

Dr. Bianco asked me to let him rebuild Oogy's face. He informed me he had never before performed facial reconstructive surgery to the extent Oogy needed it, but at the same time, he had every confidence in his ability to successfully complete the procedure. Although the scope of damage and deformity presented a great challenge, Dr. Bianco assured me that when the procedure had been completed, Oogy's life would be better than it currently was. Dr. Bianco also promised me that when he was done, Oogy would be the "Brad Pitt of dogdom."

Our confidence in Dr. Bianco's surgical skills was such that we had no doubt of the outcome — the operation would be a complete success. I think one reason we felt this way was that we knew the surgery was something Dr. Bianco *wanted* to do for Oogy's well-being.

In what turned out to be a three-and-a-half-hour operation, Dr. Bianco first removed all the scar tissue down to the muscle. Later, he told me that after all the scar tissue was taken out, there was a hole in Oogy's head the size of a softball. He held up a closed fist to give me some idea of the extent. Next, Dr. Bianco took off the remaining stump of an ear and all the skin surrounding it that had become embedded with scar tissue. He undermined the skin — removed its attachment to the underlying muscle — in

154

order to allow it to reattach naturally instead of by adhering to the scar tissue. Dr. Bianco then pulled up a flap of skin from Oogy's neck and joined it to the fur on the back of his muzzle with skin grafts he removed from the insides of his front legs. During this part of the surgery, Dr. Bianco's chief concern was that there might not be enough skin to complete the reconstructive process, but there was. Next, because covering a natural opening might lead to problems with postoperative draining, Dr. Bianco located the spot where Oogy's left ear had been and made a small hole in the side of Oogy's cranium. He then created an artificial horizontal canal into Oogy's skull from the little hole that was now all that was left of Oogy's ear. This would help avoid infection postsurgery. Dr. Bianco did not bother to replicate the vertical canal that had been torn out when Oogy had been attacked, since Oogy would never be able to hear from this ear no matter what.

The day after the surgery, I was allowed to visit Oogy in the hospital portion of the building. This was a special privilege I was given only because the patient was Oogy. The left side of Oogy's face was swollen and distorted, and he appeared bruised, as though he had been beaten. A black line of fine stitches ran down the left side of his face, which had been shaved down to his baby pink skin; a second, horizontal line of stitches helped stabilize the flaps of flesh that had been joined. There were blue gauze wraps on his forelegs, protecting the spots where the skin had been removed for the grafts. There was a Penrose drain in his head that ran from the upper left quadrant of his skull and came out the underside of his jaw. Blood and some clear, viscous fluid continually seeped out of the bottom of the drain. He looked more forlorn than any dog should ever have to be. He slept in the largest cage the hospital had, but it was still a cage, and I knew it created anxiety for him. Yet the accommodations were unavoidable, and although before the operation I could not have envisioned what he would look like, the surgery clearly had proved to be a complete success. He no longer looked terrifying (I'm not sure a dog with one ear can ever be described as normal-looking), but more important, the fact that the pressure that had been exerted by the expanded scar tissue was now eliminated meant he would finally be able to go through his days without chronic pain. We had to look at "the big picture," and although I felt bad for Oogy in that moment, I knew that the experience would have no permanently negative effect on his disposition.

I was allowed to visit him every day, and each day he grew stronger. He wore an E-collar, a clear plastic protective device that radiated outward from his neck. (Its name is derived from the ruffs Elizabethan men sported atop their tunics.) This was to prevent Oogy from scratching, biting, and licking at the sutures. It made Oogy look like a 1950s-style space doggy. I would let him out of his cage and spend as much time as I could spare sitting on the floor next to him, trying to stay out of the way of the staff as they performed their duties. Oogy would curl up next to me while I read a book or magazine with one hand and stroked him gently with the other; it was the best I could do to try to encourage and to calm him. The fact that he was sedated with painkillers no doubt helped to reduce the stress that resulted from being away from us, from having to sleep in a steel box, and from the demands of the surgery itself. Although I could see in his face and read in his body language that he was miserable, he never indicated any anxiety or discomfort.

He trusted us. All of us.

Once he was allowed to come home, Oogy still had to wear the E-collar. In almost comical fashion, he walked into doorjambs with it and banged it on walls or against cabinets, eventually cracking it into pieces. I replaced it with a somewhat smaller one so that he would have less trouble navigating the house. We removed the E-collar when Oogy ate, and after several days, we would remove the collar when we were sitting with him. This allowed him to feel more comfortable, and if he started to scratch or lick his stitches, we could stop him and put the collar back on. Before we went to sleep, we would put it on him for the night.

Ten days after the surgery, Ardmore removed the stitches. The white fur was growing back.

Oogy's face is an unavoidable, constant reminder of what he has had to endure. His face *is* what he has had to endure. Now there is a small black hole where Oogy's left ear used to be. On the right side of his head, the undamaged side, his coat is feathered behind the ear. On the left side, however, where the skin of his neck has been pulled forward, the feathering is just behind his eye and in front of where the ear would be if he had one. Instead of being smooth and seamless, the line of feathering on his left side is ragged and slightly raised, like an aerial photograph of sea foam washing up on a shoreline. This is actually the line that represents where the two parts of Oogy's face were sewn together. It runs from the top of his skull to the underside of his jaw. Because part of his jawbone had been broken off, removing support for Oogy's facial structure, the shape of his face shifted as he grew. In addition, the flesh and muscle on that side of his forehead atrophied from lack of blood flow, gradually causing the left side of the top of Oogy's skull to slope downward, whereas the left side of his face has been pulled slightly upward from the surgeries. As a result, he appears lopsided. His right upper jowl hangs below his lower jaw in normal fashion, but his left one does not; his left eye is not parallel to his right eye but is slightly higher on his face and somewhat larger. The left side of his large black nose angles upward while the right side does not. Viewed straight on, he looks like a portrait that has been torn in half but not quite properly aligned before being taped back together. This misshapen visage has also given him what one woman described as "a permanent smile." It's there, especially from the front, a slight turnup at the corner of his mouth, as though he is hearing some subtle, wry joke to which no one else is privy. The flesh where his muzzle and neck have been joined feels slightly corrugated.

Because a piece of his jaw is missing, there is not enough bone for his lower lip, a piece of which hangs down like a tiny valance. As a result of the ever-present moisture from inside his mouth, this part of his lip collects all kinds of dust, food, and other detritus that dries into a stiff paste. We routinely remove the gook that collects on the part of his lip where it hangs down. It is as natural to us as petting him. I have told the boys that when they are older, they will recall these reflexive, habitual acts of kindness with great fondness. It is the kind of unique act of loving intimacy that helps forge the connection and the bond. Oogy hates the sensation of having his lip cleaned because we literally have to pull the muck off of him like adhesive tape, but he seems to appreciate the fact that we are willing to do so.

Early one evening during the summer of the year that

Oogy's face was rebuilt, he came hobbling into the house from one of his routine forays out in the yard. He could not put any weight at all on his right rear leg. It was drawn up tight, almost as though it had been suddenly compressed. He hobbled in on the other three and made it as far as the hallway, where he collapsed. All that he could manage to do was lie there, panting. He did not moan or whimper or otherwise vocalize, but his inability to put any weight on his leg was a testament to the pain he was in. He even coughed up some yellow bile. I had some sedatives left over from the prior surgery. I fed him a dose in a piece of meat, and although he would not eat anything more, this helped him to sleep.

That night, I slept on the floor next to him. I knew that if I didn't, he would risk further injury by climbing up the stairs to be with me, since the boys were away at camp. As much as I was trying to protect him from hurting himself, I was also doing it to make myself feel better, because there was nothing more that I could do for him. I had no pain medicine to give him. As early as I could get Dr. Bianco to see him, I picked Oogy up and carried him to the van, then shot over to the hospital. Ordinarily, Oogy would start whining and yelping when he got within six blocks of the hospital. This time, he lay curled on the floor for the entire trip.

Once we arrived at the hospital, I lifted him out of the van and lugged him up the steps. Inside, he lay on the floor at my feet, panting. When Dr. Bianco appeared, two of the technicians carried Oogy into one of the examination rooms. Dr. Bianco did some manipulations with the leg. "It's a torn ACL," he informed me.

"A torn what?" I asked.

"Ligament—his anterior cruciate ligament, or what's generally called the ACL," he explained. "He tore it."

"How'd he do that?" I wondered.

"Who knows? He could have been running in your yard and stepped in a hole. It's going to have to be surgically repaired."

"Can you fix it?" I asked.

"No," Dr. Bianco said. "Unfortunately, compared to the type of surgery Oogy needs, what I do is remove warts."

Dr. Bianco recommended a hospital some forty minutes away where a specialist performed ACL reconstructive surgery. "With smaller dogs they can actually replace the ACL with fishing line," he explained. "But given the muscles in Oogy's leg, this is going to require special surgery. This guy is not cheap, but he's the best there is. It doesn't pay to take any chances, especially with a dog as massive and as special as this one."

It was enough for me that Dr. Bianco had recommended this surgeon as the best option under the circumstances. There was never a question that he always had Oogy's best interests at heart.

"How much is it going to cost?" I asked. "Do you have any idea?"

"I'm not sure. Probably around fifteen hundred to two thousand dollars."

I called the hospital and made an appointment. Oogy was evaluated that same afternoon and scheduled for surgery on the next day. When I met with the surgeon, he exchanged no pleasantries or small talk with me. He appeared to exhibit no interest in the animal before him. He explained how he would saw down the bones and then use steel plates that would be screwed into the bones to hold them together. He showed me the X-rays of Oogy's leg and drawings of what the procedure would involve. The actual cost of the surgery was almost double what Dr. Bianco had anticipated. On the drive home, I battled the feeling that I had failed Oogy. I had told him that I would do everything in my power not to let anything bad happen to him again. While I had known that such a pledge would be difficult to uphold, it had never occurred to me that it might be impossible.

Late in the afternoon of the next day, the surgeon called to let me know everything had gone well. The hospital kept Oogy another two days for observation. After twenty-four hours, however, I was allowed to come for a short visit. I went into one of the examination rooms, and after a few minutes Oogy came hobbling out, wearing another E-collar. I sat next to him on the floor—I always feel more comfortable in such moments if I am on his level—and he put his head in my lap. I fought back tears, I felt so bad for him. It just seemed never to end. A jagged pink scar ran several inches down the outside of his right leg, held together by a number of tiny black stitches. I wanted Oogy to think of better things; I wanted to soothe him. I tried to think of songs, but I forgot the words to everything. Then I started to softly speak some of the words of a poem that inexplicably popped into my head, one an old friend had recited to win a contest back in sixth grade. It was rhythmic, and though I could remember only the first of the verses, as I started to speak, Oogy's tail began to wag. I repeated the lines several times. Maybe it was simply the tone of my voice, but it really seemed to relax him.

I hated the drive home that afternoon.

When I returned to pick him up the next day, I was told to keep him sedated and give him some painkillers for the next week. The surgeon also told me that Oogy was allowed very limited exercise, several walks a day in the yard and always on a leash. There was to be no running, jumping, or climbing, and I was to confine him in the house to a six-foot-by-ten-foot room for the next two to three months.

"There's no way that'll happen," I told the doctor. "He'll shred the door."

"Well," the doctor said, "do the best you can."

I set Oogy up in the dining room. The sun streamed through the glass wall, which made the room nice and warm, just the way he liked it. His favorite chair (which had actually become so covered with Oogy fur that it even *looked* like him) was in there. I closed the doors leading to the hallway. I brought in his water dish; I also brought in his bone blanket, spread it over the rug, and laid a bone on top of it for him. I made sure he was comfortable. Then I looked at the swinging door leading to the kitchen, trying to figure out what I could place against it that would prevent him from pushing it open. That's when it dawned on me that he might try to push against it if he felt he could move it at all, which might lead to more problems than it prevented. Since it was a swinging door, I'd have to effectively block both sides lest he try to pull it open from the dining room. So I figured, Okay, he can access the kitchen, too, and I left that door open and closed the door leading from the kitchen into the hallway. Then I said good-bye and went to the office for a few hours.

When I returned home, I found Oogy sleeping on the dining room table.

The boys were away at camp for the rest of that week. Night came, and Jennifer eventually went up to bed. Earlier that evening, I had cut a piece of plywood the width of the stairs. I slid this into place between two of the ban-

ister newels to block Oogy's access to the second floor
and followed Jennifer upstairs. No sooner had I climbed
into bed than I heard Oogy's whine, followed quickly by
a crashing noise. Within seconds, Oogy was standing
next to the bed, wagging his tail and asking for attention.
He had leapt over the plywood barrier. It was apparent
that the only way to keep him from using the stairs was
for me to sleep with him on the first floor. I gathered up a
comforter and walked very slowly downstairs with him. I
placed the comforter and a pillow on the family room
floor, then lay down about three-quarters of the way to
the right side of the comforter. I knew from prior experience that as I would move in my sleep, Oogy would move
with me and that it was essentially impossible to get him
to move back so I could reclaim my own space. Oogy
curled up next to me, and we both eventually dozed off.

Luckily, it was summer, so it was not a problem when
Oogy needed to go out in the night. Oogy and I would
slowly circle the yard once or twice under a canopy of
stars—just the two of us and a few owls alive in our part
of the world, watching the blinking lights of a plane
slowly traversing the sky overhead, listening to the occasional passage of distant vehicles, all the flowers, red and
yellow and white, now colorless in the clearing in front of
the hedges.

I slept in the family room for the rest of the week,

until the boys came home from camp. It was the only way to make certain that Oogy wouldn't try to climb the stairs. I slept on the floor, not on a couch, because I knew that Oogy would climb onto the couch to sleep alongside me, putting pressure on the recently repaired joint. When the boys came home, they readily took over the job of sleeping downstairs with Oogy. They saw this partly as a responsibility that they felt they were better equipped to handle than their old dad and partly as a cool adventure. But when Oogy needed to go outside, he would go to the back door and start whining and barking. And I was always the one who heard him—the boys slept deeply—and the one who would accompany him. It was neither an imposition nor a demand. He needed me. And it enabled me to feel good about myself. I enjoyed being relied upon and being able to help.

As it turned out, the boys' willingness to sleep downstairs was the start of another phase of their lives. They never moved back upstairs into their own rooms. It didn't take long for them to realize that it was actually teenage boy heaven down there. For years after Oogy had ruined the two Chesterfield sofas, there was nothing much in the formal living room, with its manteled fireplace and brass wall sconces supporting hurricane lamp electric lights, and we rarely used it. Then, slowly, it mutated into more of a recreation room than anything else. We put a ping-pong table in there, then a wide-screen TV that Jennifer was given as a gift for some environmental work she did for a client, and an Xbox 360 soon followed. There was also a wide-screen TV in the family room, and a DVD player in each room. What wasn't there was just as essential to the downstairs experience: Jennifer and I were *upstairs* and could not listen to phone calls, ask about text messages, or tell the boys to turn off the TV or get off the computer and *get to sleep*.

Upstairs, where both boys slept from the time they were three until they turned fifteen, their rooms have been frozen in time like broken clocks. The sports trophies they earned throughout their elementary and middle school years line the windowsills in both rooms. Bookcases are filled with books that haven't been opened in years. In and on top of the dressers are clothes that will never be worn again and stuffed animals that have been abandoned. The only recent additions are some athletic plaques and awards from high school, as well as some newspaper clippings recounting their victories in sports.

Following his ACL operation, Oogy was permitted only one form of exercise: walking around the yard. We did this routinely in the morning and evening, and I would come home at least once during the middle of the day for a third go-round; otherwise, his leg would stiffen up on him. Weekends, I added one or two more of these strolls. In addition, I massaged his knee every morning before work and every evening before bed. Ardmore eventually took out the stitches.

Several weeks after the operation to repair his ACL, Oogy's right knee became swollen and hot to the touch. He began limping again. He was running a fever and lost his appetite. Dr. Bianco examined the leg and determined that Oogy had developed a postoperative infection. I made an appointment for that same afternoon and took Oogy back to the surgeon, who ascertained that Oogy's body had rejected the steel implants that were holding his leg together. The surgeon told me he could prescribe an antibiotic that would knock down the infection, but he was certain it would return as soon as Oogy stopped taking the medicine. He said the only sensible course was, unfortunately, to open up Oogy's leg again, take off the plates that were in place, and use a different kind of support. That was going to cost another fifteen hundred dollars. I considered contesting the charge since I'd had nothing to do with the decision to put that type of plate on Oogy's leg, but I realized it was not worth antagonizing the man who was going to perform the surgery. Besides, how could I prove that the decision had been medically unwise?

Oogy spent another three days at the hospital, and when at last he returned home, we started the rehabilitative process all over again.

After this surgery, Dr. Bianco advised that it was important to keep Oogy's weight down to reduce stress on the repaired joint. He prescribed a diet dry food that was specially formulated to provide joint lubrication. Ever since then, Oogy hasn't had a bite of canned dog food. Twice a day I've fed him half a cup of dry, all-natural dog food made from organic vegetables with some chicken added in, mixed with half a cup of the prescription dry food. Neither of these has any noticeable fat content. With breakfast, he also gets a pill that is an over-the-counter lubricant for his joints, fish oil for his coat, and Ester-C for his overall health. Dinner is the same food ration without the pills, but I sprinkle on some powder made of shark cartilage. This supplement is hailed as a joint lubricant, but it also makes me feel like a sort of witch doctor: I do not know for certain that it helps, but I want to believe that it will make things easier for him.

When a month had passed, the surgeon announced that the healing had progressed to the point where Oogy could safely begin water therapy. He explained that swimming would allow Oogy to exercise his leg without straining it and would increase the rate at which his flexibility returned. The doctor told me there were two locations in the area where dogs could be taken to swim. His staff gave me the numbers, and I called both places. Knowing that Oogy disliked the feel of water on his body and that he also hated to be confined, I had a strong suspicion that he was not going to be an easy patient.

When I arrived at the facility I had decided to use, a staff member greeted me and we walked into the building that housed the exercise pool. An older dog had just exited the pool, and his owner was toweling him down. The staff member explained in a quiet voice that the dog had a degenerative spinal disease.

The staff member bent over and clasped an inflated vest on Oogy, pulling it on over his front legs. Velcro straps held the vest together on Oogy's back, and we attached two yellow horse leads, each about twelve feet long, to rings on either side of the vest. Then we each took one of the leads and, with one of us on either side of the pool, slowly walked forward and drew a very reluctant Oogy down the steps and into the water. Oogy began to resist more actively. The staff member called over to say that Oogy would get used to it. As we guided him off the steps and into the pool itself, Oogy seemed instead to panic and flounder, inhaling large gulps of water, thrashing furiously. I saw that he was very afraid, and I could not allow that to continue. I had reached *my* discomfort level in seconds.

"Let's get him out!" I said, and we pulled Oogy back to the steps. Oogy was panting laboriously; he seemed exhausted and was clearly terribly shaken.

I was told that many dogs reacted like Oogy the first

time they went in. But it did not make any difference to me what other dogs' experiences had been: I couldn't and didn't want to subject Oogy to further torment. However, because the surgeon had recommended swim therapy, I thought that we should try it at least one more time to see if there was any way to reduce his fear.

There wasn't. The second visit was my last. I knew I would have to try something else. Even if there was a therapeutic benefit to this experience from a physical standpoint, the emotional reaction it was causing Oogy would cancel it out, and he had already had enough of being afraid in his life. I could not allow myself to cause him any more fear. I remembered the promise I had made. I would just have to find another option.

So I went back to Dr. Bianco, who recommended a recently opened facility nearby that provided grooming services as well as physiotherapy for small animals. I made an appointment and drove over there. My first impression was that it was a rather tony little spa catering to wealthy Main Line pet owners. But, as with so many things in life, only part of that picture was accurate.

The facility certainly was, in part, a tony little spa catering to wealthy Main Line pet owners. It was also a superior rehabilitative facility. A vet who specialized in pet rehabilitative medicine assessed Oogy's needs at the time of his initial visit. She prescribed a series of treatments involving electronic stimulation of his atrophied muscle as well as hydrotherapy. The woman who administered these treatments had a specialized degree in pet physiotherapy. But actually giving Oogy the hydrotherapy treatments presented a problem. The hydrotherapy is administered in a clear Lucite box, open at the top, with a treadmill as the box's floor. Warm water is gradually introduced while the treadmill turns at an incrementally increasing speed, so that the dog is eventually trotting with resistance that, over time, will build up the muscle without stressing it. Oogy, however, panicked when he was shut into the box, even a clear one without a top.

After I explained what underlay this response, the therapist started very gradually to increase Oogy's time in the box with each visit (without charging us for it). As soon as Oogy started to become afraid, she stopped the procedure, no matter what stage it was in, and let him out. She also quickly hit on the creative solution of putting another dog in the box with him. Since all the women who worked there had at least one dog—the therapist herself had two ridgebacks that, big as he is, Oogy could practically walk under—and all the dogs knew him, finding a companion dog was never a problem. After six visits, Oogy was able to embark stress-free on his course of therapy. The mass and tone of his leg returned, as did its resiliency.

More than results matter in relationships with animals. How you get to where you need to go is critically important. The calm, loving approach exhibited by the staff at the rehab facility gave me a sense of confidence in the healing process. Oogy responded profoundly to the latter. And if I was late in picking him up, or a prior session was running late when we arrived, Oogy was used as a greeter to make other dogs feel welcomed. Here, as at AAH, the staff put the welfare of the animals in their care above any other consideration.

One afternoon as we were leaving after Oogy's session, the owner of a local rescue service was bringing in a dog. As it turned out, the spa also donated its services for dogs from his rescue and cleaned them up before they went to their new homes.

As soon as he saw Oogy, he asked, "Is that a Dogo?"

"Well done," I said. "You're like the fourth person I've met who recognized the breed."

"What happened to him?"

"He was a bait dog," I explained.

"God bless you," he said.

"You know, I think that is the first time in my life anyone has ever said that to me without my having to sneeze first," I replied.

Right after Oogy's operation, the surgeon had cautioned me that it is essentially inevitable that once a dog tears one ACL, he will tear the other, because he will favor the undamaged leg. A little over a year after his first ACL injury, Oogy started limping again. It was much less pronounced than it had been the last time, and Dr. Bianco could not find anything wrong even when, while Oogy was sedated for a minor operation, he manipulated the leg Oogy was favoring. The X-rays showed nothing, either. But the problem did not disappear. So after a few days of this, and realizing that just because he showed no pain did not mean he was not feeling any, I took Oogy back out to the surgeon. He merely glanced at Oogy's gait when he came into the examination room.

"He's got a slow tearing of the ACL going on," the doctor said with complete assurance.

"You can tell that just from looking at him?" I asked somewhat incredulously.

"*I* can tell that," the doctor said. I appreciated his confidence because it underscored his expertise. And then he added, "I'm terribly sorry this happened. But now there won't be any more."

He was trying to make me feel better instead of treating me impersonally, as though this were an unemotional business transaction. For the first time, he had expressed some sympathy and had made an effort to connect. I felt better about him as a result.

Oogy had his second ACL surgically repaired—and

again, he developed a postoperative infection that took him back to the hospital for several days of treatment to knock down the fever and treat the infection. The second surgery, however, was most memorable not for the procedure, but for a conversation I had with a technician there.

When the tech who was bringing Oogy out so I could take him home entered the waiting room, I got down on the floor to say hello to my dog. The tech said to me, "This is a great dog. A great dog. He's loving, he's gentle, and he's really, really smart."

While Oogy licked me repeatedly as if he were saying "Hello" and "Thank you for being here" and "I can't wait to get home," I said in an offhand fashion, "Isn't that kind of a contradiction when it comes to dogs?"

The tech's eyes narrowed. "Listen," he said to me. There was a real sternness in his tone of voice. "You don't understand. I see hundreds of dogs each month, and every once in a while there's one of them that's really special. And you've got him."

When I took Oogy to Ardmore to have his stitches removed, I related this conversation to Dr. Bianco. Initially, I thought he might not have heard me. His attention remained on the task he was performing.

Then, without looking up from his ministrations, he said, "But we already knew that."

CHAPTER  *Signs*

It sometimes feels like destiny that we were at the hospital that Saturday morning because of Buzzy's illness, but Diane revealed to me years later that as soon as she was certain that Oogy would survive, once she had completed fostering him and knew he was adoptable, she had decided to call me to ask if I would take in this pup they had saved who had only one ear. So at some point, our phone would have rung and Oogy would have been waiting at the other end, not unlike how Noah and Dan had been waiting for us years before. The inescapable conclusion is that Oogy was meant to be here.

There are other things that make me feel that Oogy's involvement in our lives was preordained. Several likenesses of Oogy existed in our house for years before we actually met him. Long before the boys were born, when Jennifer and I actually had some disposable income as well as free time to travel, we happened upon an art gallery in Vancouver that specialized in Inuit art. Over three separate visits there in the next five years, we collected a number of Inuit prints for the house. One of them, which has been in our first-floor hallway for the past fifteen years, and had been in our old house for five years before that, is called *My Dog Protecting Me*. It shows two small white dogs in the foreground, each of which has the arm of an Inuit man in its jaw. In the background, two larger versions of the dogs in the foreground are standing on hind legs with their paws on two other Inuit men. In the center of these four figures is the face of another Inuit man. Each half of his face is looking in a different direction at one of the dog-man pairings. The two large dogs look exactly like Oogy. They have the same prominent snouts and stocky bodies, the same muscular rear haunches. They are standing on their hind legs the same way Oogy often does. I am not sure which dog is protecting whom, or from what, but my sense is that the four dogs actually represent one single dog and that they are protecting the man with two faces. This print has always spoken to me of the best of bonds between people and dogs, and looking at it has never failed to give me an appreciation of that relationship. Given the level of devotion Oogy exhibits toward us and the physical similarities he shares with the dogs in this print, it is almost as though he has stepped out of that picture and come to life—and perhaps this is why I felt I recognized him when I first met him.

A second prescient picture cropped up years later in an entirely different context. When the boys were in seventh grade and Oogy had already been with us for a year, Dan did some research on our house for a school project. We live in the original farmhouse in our neighborhood, a part of which is about one hundred and fifty years old. Among the things Dan learned was that a former owner of the property, a veterinarian, began buying up small amounts of acreage from various neighbors until he owned about two hundred acres. During his research, Dan found a picture, which appears to have been taken in the 1930s, of the veterinarian's son standing in front of a cornfield next to a white dog. The boy is wearing an Irish-style cap, a plaid sweater vest, and knickers. And the dog looks *exactly* the way Oogy would if he had both ears. Something about that fact has always resonated with me—that before any of us was alive, a dog that looked just like Oogy lived here.

These pictures, both strikingly similar representations of Oogy, one frozen in time eighty years past not far from where Oogy sleeps now, the other from an artist's imagination twenty-five years ago, create a continuity of Oogy in our house, pre-dating his actual presence by decades. I hear Oogy echoing down the halls of time and back again like magic. He has been here for a long, long while.

When he was just over a year old and we were having trouble coping with Oogy's energy, we hired a trainer at the recommendation of a friend. The trainer, our friend told us, claimed to be able to talk to animals, but she herself was skeptical. The morning the trainer came for her first visit, I introduced her to Oogy, who was lying on his blanket in the family room. The trainer sat on the floor next to him for a full five minutes. Jennifer, Noah, Dan, and I stood just outside the doorway to the room, in the hallway, watching the trainer bend and put her head next to Oogy's, watching her lips move next to his ear; then she would pull back a few inches and focus her gaze on him before leaning forward to whisper to him again. The four of us were exchanging skeptical glances with one another. We could not hear a word she said—or anything Oogy said back to her, for that matter. We had hired the woman to train Oogy, not to talk to him.

When the trainer lifted her head after her discussion was complete, her eyes were brimming with tears. "Oogy wants you to know," she said, "how much he appreciates the love and respect you've shown him."

We were not sure how to react to this statement. We could understand the truth of what she said, of course. It made sense he would have felt that way. But the statement presented a number of possibilities. Had Oogy actually communicated that to her telepathically? Or, because the trainer could see that Oogy was well loved and could also see he had been abused in the past, was she simply making a logical deduction? In the end, though, I realized that it didn't matter—the important thing was that she had learned this about Oogy. Even if she was only stating the obvious, the obvious was noteworthy.

The trainer then asked about Oogy's daily routine. I started by taking her across the hall and showing her the crate where Oogy stayed when we left the house. I didn't mention that Oogy resisted being put in the box, nor did I describe how he barked incessantly once he was confined. The trainer looked at the crate and without a moment's hesitation turned to me and said, "You've got to get him out of that box."

"Why?" I asked.

"Because," she said, "Oogy associates being in a crate with having his ear ripped off."

It was a smack-myself-in-the-forehead moment. In my ignorance, I had attributed Oogy's abhorrence of the crate to his frustration and anxiety at being separated from us. From that day on, Oogy never went back in the crate, which for him had represented a fundamental fear that he had had to confront on a daily basis. I felt awful that, even inadvertently, I had caused Oogy some fear. I should have known by his incessant barking that something was amiss, but I had not understood the reason. I had completely misjudged the level of distress this had caused him. The trainer's intuitive grasp of this truth earned her my immediate respect and gratitude.

The experience with the trainer also had a wholly unintended and beneficial consequence for me. I began paying attention to how Oogy communicated not only with me, but with other people as well.

The pictures that suggest Oogy's presence in our lives before he arrived, even the events that created a sense of inevitability that his life would be commingled with ours, are also a form of message. But on a daily basis, I pass messages to Oogy, both nonverbally and verbally, though not always in literal fashion, and he, in his own fashion, speaks to me.

There is some language-specific interaction. Although I was skeptical at first, I no longer doubt that Oogy understands certain specific words. For example, when I use the words *dog park* in a sentence, he gets very excited. I keep telling him that he can't understand me when I say that, but his behavior contradicts this. It's an association he has not with time of day (we go at different times) or with an action (like picking up the keys), but with the words I actually use.

There are also behavior-specific things I do that tell Oogy something. When I take off the collar for the invisible fence, he understands immediately that he is going somewhere. In the morning, when I put on my shoes, he knows that I am leaving and goes to his hiding spot underneath the dining room table as though he can somehow avoid the inevitable. His sadness is as palpable as a finger in my eye.

There are also times, even if I'm just talking nonsense to him, that he clearly grasps the feelings that my gibberish is meant to convey. The content is irrelevant; it is the emotions I'm sharing with him, through the tone of my voice or my affect, that speak to and comfort him.

For example, one Friday evening this past summer, while we were in the midst of an extended heat spell, I cooked Oogy some bones. This particular day had been over one hundred degrees. At ten in the evening, it was still steaming, the air thick with moisture. In the darkness outside, the sound of cicadas swelled and ebbed. Our house does not have central air-conditioning, and although the exterior walls are eighteen inches thick, the relative coolness the house can retain on the first floor had long since been baked out by the sustained pounding the heat had given us over the week. The boys were in the family room, where there is an air conditioner, watching TV. Oogy was sleeping on the floor next to them. Jennifer was out at the gym. And I was in the kitchen. I had ten small bones that I had baked for Oogy in the toaster oven and needed to put into the freezer. Oogy usually gets at least one bone each day. He prefers small bones; with his shattered jaw, he cannot grip large ones.

I put the bones into a bag and sealed it, and as I was placing the bag in the freezer, I saw Oogy standing in the entrance to the kitchen, staring at me. There was no light on in the eating area; the kitchen itself was only dimly lit. I had not heard him come in. It was as though he had been teleported. Some alarm only he could hear had sounded, awakening him. The food Klaxon was gonging away: "Food alert! There is food in sector K-2. Repeat! Food in sector K-2!" The aroma of cooked meat had wafted down the hall, curling into his nose like a feathery hook; it had awakened him and caused him to rise, leading him to pad down to where he now stood. Or maybe he heard me opening the bag, the rustling sound familiar to him, significant. "I'm here," he seemed to say to me. "What am I missing? Do I get anything to eat? Why didn't you tell me there was food available?"

In response, the first thing I said to him was, "You're a Dogo. The Dogo is a sturdy breed with a prominent black nose. I learned that tonight. You have a prominent black nose. Did you know that?"

His face was expressionless. He was looking for more information.

"You just missed it," I told him. "You just missed the Ceremony of the Bones, when we place the baked bones into the freezer following the designs of an ancient ritual. Now, they are safely ensconced in the bowels of the freezer. However, I can tell you that later on tonight one very lucky dog will get at least one of the bones. After the Opening of the Freezer Door ritual. And," I said, dropping my voice to barely a whisper, "confidentially, I have it on good authority that will be you." I nodded at him, kissed him on the top of his skull, rubbed both sides of his head behind his ear and the unear, feeling the rough line of scar tissue that holds his face together.

"You're a big baby dog," I told him. I could see clearly the flap of flesh that had been his neck in the shadows playing on him, how it had been pulled forward and attached to what had remained of his face. "You're a folded dog," I said. "Do not fold, bend, spindle, or mutilate. Isn't that how it goes?" He looked at me. His expression did not change. He stood perfectly still, tolerating my idiocy. And then I said, "Oops. Too late for you."

I had no idea where these words were coming from,

but I was sure he understood what lay behind them even if I did not. Just as I understand him. Because Oogy also talks to me.

Sometimes we are sitting together and I am reading or working on the laptop when he will start pawing and whining at me to notice him. There are times he will move off the couch where we are sitting together and start growling, demanding that I come to where *he* is and pay attention to him. "Do you want to go out?" I'll ask him. "Do you want a bone? Do you want some attention? Come here." Then he'll bark at me. He wants me on his level. It's that simple. So I will uncoil from the couch and lie down next to him, stroke him, and the murmurings cease; he has the attention he has asked me for.

As he has matured, Oogy's ability to express his desire both for attention and for affection has evolved. I don't really understand the source of his perception. It may be instinctual, a product of the years he and I have spent together emotionally committed to each other unclouded by the white noise—the relentless clatter and superficiality—that courses through the daily lives of human beings. Or it just may be that he comprehends much more speech than I give him credit for or can intuit signs from daily activities that I wouldn't notice.

The first time this happened, he woke me at 6:00 on a Saturday morning. That evening, I would be going overseas for business. I had not taken out my suitcase or begun packing yet, so Oogy could not have had any apparent clue that I was going away. When I heard him come upstairs and he whined once and stuck that cold, wet nose in my face, I reacted by first asking him if he wanted to join me on the bed, hoping he wasn't expecting me to go downstairs and let him out. I patted the mattress several times, but he made no move to join me. Instead, his hind legs danced sideways back and forth, and he continued to whine at me, never taking his eyes off my face. Then, resigned, I asked him if he needed to go out, and since he did not want to sleep next to me, I realized he did. I threw back the covers and followed him. Expecting that he would head to the back door, when we arrived on the first floor I turned left from the stairs and started in that direction. But instead of heading to the kitchen and access to the yard, Oogy went into the room to the right of the stairway where Dan was sleeping and climbed onto the couch. He sat there, waiting for me, looking directly at me. He wanted me to sit next to him. So I wormed my way onto the sofa, lifted up Dan's feet, marveling at the thick blond hair curling over his legs, and slid underneath them, putting them on my lap. I was able to pull a part of the comforter over me. Dan never stirred. Oogy curled up between us and put his head on my lap, and as I rubbed his back and luxuriated in his warmth, he turned his head to look at me with utter adoration in his eyes, the ragged line that delineates where his face was sewn together defined in shadow by the light from the windows. We slept that way for another two hours.

Later that afternoon, when I started packing, Oogy came into the room and lay on the bed the entire time. Only when I had closed the suitcase, stood up, picked up the bag, and started downstairs did he jump off the bed and trail after me, following me from room to room until it was time for me to leave for the airport. Clearly, he somehow understood that I was going away and wanted to be around me as much as he could before then.

I am not, of course, the only person Oogy communicates with. Although neither Jennifer nor the boys have developed the same degree of intimacy with him given the demands of their daily routines, messages do pass back and forth between them. And his being, his visage, and his loving temperament, despite the destruction so obviously visited upon him, draw in person after person we meet outside the house. Because Oogy is much more than a unique personality and a loving pet. Who he is and what he has endured speaks to people.

A woman I know who is a columnist and author, and

has been involved in animal rescue for decades on the West Coast, recently said to me, "Stories about fighting dogs that have happy endings are rare. Stories about fighting dogs that are inspirational are nonexistent."

I have often wondered what exactly it is about Oogy that resonates with people. To a certain extent, each person has his or her own connection with him. Some appreciate Oogy's demeanor; the word *sweet* has been used to describe him more than any other. When they have learned what he has gone through and have seen how he is in spite of it, people are simply moved by his resiliency, his placid dignity. In some people, I think, a certain degree of transference is inevitable as they come to see in Oogy the survivor they perceive themselves to be, an indomitable spirit in the face of adversity. Others, not necessarily physically damaged but emotionally scarred, who yet hope still to be loved, find another kind of encouragement: If this dog can go through the hell he did and emerge capable of giving and generating as much love as he does, so can they. His triumph over the most unspeakable brutality without any emotional ill effects whatsoever encourages many. And, I think, some people just appreciate the second chance Oogy has had, just as they hope they will get theirs if and when they need one.

But there is an element common to everyone who connects with him, and it took me a very long time to arrive at what that is. For most of us, life represents a balancing act among a series of highs and lows, the struggle to maintain equanimity in the face of so many polarities of experience. But no matter where we reside on this spectrum, all of us know that we will, eventually and without fail, have to deal with tragedy. People we care about disappear from our lives. Animals we love have to be "put to sleep." (How's that for a euphemism to help us deal with the loss?) Loved ones die and drift apart; illness eats up family members and friends in awful ways. Every day we stand an increased chance that our lives will in some way be diminished. And what appeals to everyone about Oogy is that he is proof that what we all know is lurking out there—the awful and, yes, inevitable tragic loss, the unexplainable savage attack, the seemingly insurmountable occurrence—can, in fact, be survived with love and grace intact, without bitterness or resentment, and with an appreciation for all that follows. Oogy is, right there in front of everyone he meets, tangible living proof that there can be happiness, love, and hope on the other side of unspeakable and unimaginable horror.

In warm weather when we go for a walk in the little nearby town of Narberth, strangers invariably approach us to meet Oogy. His appearance inspires a lot of questions. I generally try to avoid telling very young children what really happened to Oogy; I simply tell them that another dog attacked him. Because both humans and dogs had abused Oogy, strangers are unfailingly surprised that he is as gentle with animals and people as he is. When people first encounter Oogy, they invariably ask if he is safe. My stock response is, "Well, he has licked two people to death...." Waitresses, waiters, and patrons at the outdoor cafés and people eating, drinking, or catching smokes outside of the bars and restaurants swarm all over Oogy. On weekend nights, several of the regulars in downtown Narberth carry treats to give to him. Oogy enjoys the attention that he gets. I am happy for him. It is some form of compensation. I often tell people we encounter on these strolls that we're there because Oogy likes the nightlife. In a way, that's true.

It is an altogether different experience when we go to a dog park and I let Oogy run free. This has served to both expand and strengthen our communicative abilities. For years, I was reluctant to let Oogy off his leash. The idea that he might run away and be lost forever reflected my anxieties: That which we love will disappear. But eventually, at Jennifer's insistence, and knowing full well how much Oogy enjoyed socializing with other dogs, I overcame my hesitation. The end result was a mutual expression of confidence that we would always be there for each other.

The first dog park I took Oogy to was at a local nature conservancy, acres of hills and hiking trails with a creek at the bottom. Dogs were not officially allowed off leash, but people had been letting them run free there for years. The opportunity to run unhindered and exhaustively and to interact with other dogs was definitely therapeutic for Oogy. Each outing was like a playdate for a young child, stimulating and relaxing at the same time. He would come home from these outings and fall into a deep sleep, his social and physical needs sated.

It took Oogy several months before he would venture into the creek. Eventually, this became a key part of our visit. Oogy would walk in the water and drink as it meandered along. On those clear, hot days, his image reflected in the creek, the picture of Oogy and Oogy upside down in the water burned into my brain. Sometimes he would walk thirty or forty yards upstream as I followed on the footpath. I could hear him sloshing in the water but was unable to see him because of the thick bushes lining the bank, until he would eventually rejoin me on the trail. The act of separating and then reuniting had deeper implications.

To be sure, there were moments when Oogy disappeared, following some scent or movement, which proved to be just as scary for me as when I'd lost sight of Noah or Dan in a crowded store when they were young. When

Oogy would disappear, I would stand and call his name, always worried that he would not be able to discern where the sound was coming from because of his missing ear. Then, when he returned, I would always tell him not to do that again because it scared me so much.

During one visit, a mother and her three young daughters were hanging out by the creek, and I heard Oogy barking as I approached. One of the little girls had waded across the creek and climbed onto a large rock on the other side. Oogy was barking at her. The mother just got the biggest kick out of that. She sensed that Oogy was concerned because of the separation. Her own dog was sprawled on the bank by the creek, paying absolutely no attention. As soon as the mother called her daughter back to the side of the creek where the rest of her family was, Oogy quieted down.

Another time, I walked along the path and listened as Oogy splashed upcreek until finally I heard him moving toward me through the brush. I did not recognize the dog that emerged. Whose dog was this? Where was Oogy? It took a moment to realize what had happened. Oogy was completely covered in putrid slate gray mud. He smelled like a fertilizer factory. Riding home with him next to me was really a testament to my love for him. It stunk like something had been dead in the van for days.

Ordinarily when Oogy gets some mud on him it dries

quickly, and because his fur is so short, I can wipe him down with a warm towel as though he's made of vinyl. But this was altogether different. When we arrived home, the boys had to hold on to Oogy while I hosed him down. Then I took warm, wet rags with dog shampoo and cleaned him further before rinsing him down a second time and then drying him with clean rags. That removed most of the sediment—and restored our relationship.

After the township's board of commissioners imposed severe restrictions on the ability of dogs to roam the conservancy unleashed, I learned that a local cemetery allowed dogs to run free—the smell of dogs scared away gophers whose tunneling undermined the gravestones—and Oogy and I spent some time there. It was an altogether different kind of experience, without the sense of joyful abandon Oogy had experienced at the conservancy. The rolling hills of the cemetery had a dull uniformity to them. There was no creek. There was no one for him to romp with. The only times I saw other dogs there, they were too far in the distance for him to engage. We visited only four or five times, and none of the visits seemed even remotely satisfactory. It was obvious that Oogy sensed there was a difference. Walking among the graves, he never strayed. He never broke into a run. The lives of the dead, the frailty of being, a brief touch on the shoulder that we are wanted elsewhere—these were palpable. The proximity of the dead seemed a weight that neither of us could avoid.

Then, in an adjacent township, we found a legitimate dog park of some thirty acres, a place where dogs *are* permitted off leash. A small creek lies at the bottom of the park. Virtually any time of the day, dogs can be found running, fetching, rolling around, chasing each other in twos and in packs. We have been there when as many as thirty dogs were galloping across the plateau, walking, playing, dogs of every shape and size and color, breeds I had never heard of and could not have imagined. It's like doggy heaven. The dog owners are a responsible group who watch out for one another's pets. We know one another's dogs by name and give them hugs and kisses as though they were our own; throw a ball or Frisbee for someone else's dog; give water from the doggy water fountain to other people's dogs. When another dog puts his muddy paws on my shirt so that he can give me a kiss, it is never a problem. After all, I tell his owner, we're all here because we love dogs.

When Oogy plays with other dogs, they run and run in circles, wrestle, flop around. Watching Oogy barrel along makes me think of the films I have seen of old-time locomotives, the big black ones, pistoning forward. Oogy is nothing but power, all muscle and moving mass. He will run for the sheer joy of running. He has some regular friends, dogs he will invariably interact with, but on any given day there is no way to predict who will be there when we are. He has also earned the nickname "the sheriff." When a couple of dogs start mixing it up, Oogy will invariably run to the altercation and check it out, and more than once he has started backing off the aggressor dog with barks and shoves. Then, once peace has been restored, he will return to what he had been doing before.

Allowing Oogy the autonomy to wander off leash has proved to be beneficial to his sense of himself as well as to our relationship. He wanders, explores, and sniffs at things I cannot see. He will dawdle along, sheer strength and ferocity gone gentle, smelling flowers, meandering without a care under the canopy of trees and amid the tang of honeysuckle. At the park, he is very independent, while at home, he seems always to need to be around one of us.

Oogy has appreciated the confidence shown in him to be off leash and on his own. He revels in the opportunity to interact with other dogs. By letting Oogy run free and mingle, and allowing him to wander in the stillness of the woods, where the only sounds are the creek and the occasional bird, the thrumming of a frog like some bass Jew's harp, the whine of insects, we have been able to step out of and beyond the routine of our lives and in so doing have grown closer together. The trust I have placed in him and the independence he experiences have confirmed that, as with so many things, I was very, very wrong: He will never leave me.

I have told Jennifer and the boys that after I die, this is where I want my memorial service held and my ashes scattered. It is a scene of great peacefulness, happiness, and love. I have asked that Oogy's ashes accompany mine. Just the other day, when I told the boys, Noah asked if instead I wanted to be buried next to our old pets just to the left of the front door. "I don't know if we'll own our house then," I said. "And anyway," I added, "with Oogy, it's different. He and I are connected on a different plane."

They said that they understood.

CHAPTER 10 *The Rescuer*

the boys' impending departure for college will bring both big and small changes. The fundamentals of our lives will have been altered. My daily schedule now that I will not have to awaken and make the boys breakfast, the grocery list, the laundry demands, what Jennifer and I will do with the time we are not spending at games and wrestling matches each week and on weekends, all represent change. Everything will become different, some in ways I can envision and others in ways that will surprise and, no doubt, tug at me.

Although both Dan and Noah were accepted into several of the same colleges, in the end they made choices that took them thousands of miles apart. Noah received an academic scholarship to a local, highly rated college, which also has a strong lacrosse program; he will play on the team, and major in business and minor in coaching so he can coach lacrosse upon graduation. Dan decided that he wanted a different cultural experience than offered by the East Coast, and went out west. His sense of challenge and adventure has led him to declare a major in criminal justice.

How the boys will deal with the separation—from Oogy and from each other—remains to be seen.

As for me, since I will have a lot more free time than I have had in the past eighteen years (none, for the most part), I recently began the process to have Oogy certified so that he can become a therapy dog. My hope is that he will be licensed as a companion dog for hospitalized children and wounded veterans. Beyond the ordinary benefits that companion dogs provide, it makes sense to me that young people in the midst of personal struggle—battling pain, depression, and anxiety and daunted by the future before them, what they will look like, how people will react to what they look like—will be encouraged by and take some inspiration from Oogy. They will see in front of them living proof that the most agonizing and horrific events can be overcome without any lasting damage to the spirit, without harm to the ability to give and receive love. I believe that Oogy will be able to help those in need to understand that scarring, disfigurement, and trauma, whether physical or emotional, do not have to define who they are. That what is on the inside counts more than what is on the outside. That no matter what has been inflicted upon them, love and dignity are attainable.

I was talking to a nurse at the dog park and allowed that I was not sure *I* was ready for these encounters. She told me that I would quickly adjust. I have my doubts, but it made me feel better to defer to her expertise.

Before an animal receives certification as a therapy pet, he (or she) must undergo hours of obedience training, following which the dog is tested by the sponsoring organization (and in some cases the particular facility itself has more stringent standards) to prove that the candidate is calm and under his or her master's control. There are simple sit and stay tests, tests for walking on command, and one that I anticipate will be hardest for Oogy: sitting while I walk away and not moving toward me until he hears the appropriate verbal command. Some of the tests are administered while rolling carts rattle, pans are dropped, glass breaks, or other dogs pass by. Ardmore recommended a man with decades of experience who is also the author of several well-received books on training dogs. He came to the house and we spent a number of hours together, much of it just talking about people-dog relationships.

He conceded that he had not anticipated the level of disfigurement on Oogy's face. "I knew that his ear was missing," he said, "but I never would have guessed that the damage to his facial structure was so extensive."

We started the training with some game playing using a tennis ball on a knotted piece of rope. The trainer had me throw the ball and give Oogy a treat when he brought it back and gave it to me. The next two times I tried this on my own, Oogy quickly lost interest in anything but the treats in my shirt pocket and would simply stand there and stare at them. The trainer and I have not had a second session yet.

Before he left, though, the trainer said something that made *me* feel rewarded. He said that Oogy and I have a relationship based on mutual love and respect, a confidence that each will be there for the other. "You're one hundred percent bonded with your dog," he said. "There's no distinction between this dog and the rest of your life. You're in a place that we try to take dog owners to, but very few of them ever get to."

I have never felt that my family did anything special or unusual in adopting Oogy. We just happened to be there when the opportunity presented itself. We didn't do it so we could feel good about ourselves for having done it—although we have felt good about ourselves for being able to help him. We did it without thinking (well, Jennifer did the thinking for us). We met and fell completely and instantaneously in love with a dog who had had unimaginable horror inflicted upon him. We did it for the dog, a dog who was obviously special. What he had endured seemed to have put him on a different plane. And in our naïveté, we did not know that we might not be able to do what we did; that the odds were very much against allowing us to take an abused fighting dog and help him unlock the love in his heart for all living creatures.

I have heard it said that you can tell a lot about a person from his or her pet. I do not know what Oogy ends up saying about us. We do not operate on some elevated level of kindness. It is not uncommon to encounter dogs that have been adopted after they have been injured. I know several three-legged dogs from the dog parks: One was shot in a hunting accident; a car hit another; the third, a fighting dog, was found on the streets of Philadelphia with half his left rear leg missing and the bone jutting out. The owner of another dog who lost some facial structure to cancer had plastic surgery performed on it to restore his face and ability to eat properly. I know a Jack Russell terrier whose hind legs do not work: His owners place him in a little two-wheeled cart so that he can get around and call him "the million-dollar dog." I know a family who found a stray who had cigarette burns all over her body and took her in; another family adopted a dog from a breeder who planned on killing him simply because he was a runt. A woman I recently met adopts strays with major medical problems, takes out a mortgage on her house to pay for treatment, and, when she has paid off the mortgage, takes out another one for different animals.

And these are only the very small number of people whom I have come to know within my own community. They speak for a collective experience of vast proportions. At the same time, I have come to understand that what Oogy went through—the unspeakable torture he was subjected to as part of some barbaric cultural exercise—and the odds that he had to overcome to have survived at all make his story, and therefore our experience, somewhat unique. He is not the product of accidental injury, but a living symbol of an epidemic that kills thousands of dogs each year. And if there is a reason this story has a happy ending, a large part of that is because every day I think about how it began.

I also think that because they are adopted, the boys relate to Oogy on another level as well. On their eighteenth birthday, I asked Noah and Dan several more of those questions I had no way of knowing the answer to. I wondered if the fact that they are adopted had influenced their lives, and if so, how. Did they feel rescued or saved in the manner in which Oogy had been rescued? Did they think that the fact they were adopted had influenced the way they related to Oogy?

I told them I was not expecting immediate answers, to take as much time as they needed, and that whatever they wanted to say would be fine. I was not looking for anything in particular. I just wanted to know. I actually wasn't sure they would be able to answer the questions—I know I couldn't have done it when I was their age.

But they could.

Dan said that he does not sit around and think about the fact that he is adopted. "I'm aware of it, of course, but I don't dwell on it," he said. He considers it to be a component of his identity, "the same as the fact that I'm a Caucasian male. I don't sit around and think about how my life would be different if I weren't a Caucasian male. I don't think about what effect it's had on my life, either. It's who I am." He told me that he never thinks in terms of Jennifer and me not being his parents. "I mean, for the last eighteen years, except for three days, which I have no memory of, you've been my mom and dad."

Dan understands that the fact that his birth parents placed him for adoption does not mean they rejected him. He appreciates that it represents an incomparable sacrifice, an act of love not only for his benefit, but also for the benefit of total strangers. At the same time, Dan does feel that he was "in a way" saved. Not in the sense that he was in any kind of danger, the way Oogy had been, but because he has never wanted for anything and has been provided with a loving, supportive home environment and significant developmental advantages, both intellectually and athletically, that he feels certain would otherwise have been unavailable to him. Dan also thinks that this sense of feeling lucky and advantaged is related to why he is so crazed about saving animals. "I can't know how I'd have related to Oogy were I not adopted," Dan explains. "But I have to think it has affected how I feel about him. We share the same experience. We both have better lives for it. I want to help him and love him the way I have been loved and guided."

In the end, it is not the fact that he is adopted that has affected Noah, it is the act of adoption itself. "I mean," he said, "for all the things that had to have happened to get me here, to have in fact happened, I find that pretty amazing."

Just like Dan, Noah has a sincere sense of appreciation for the quality of life he has enjoyed. The friendships he has been able to develop, the academic opportunities he has been offered, the fact that we were always able to somehow pay for lacrosse camps and basketball camps and overnight camps and lacrosse clubs and individual coaching, the occasional vacations, even a trip to Paris we took when they turned thirteen—all represent advantages and experiences that he is the better for and which he feels in all likelihood he would otherwise never have had. Because of that, he thinks he is more thankful for what he has been offered than someone who is not adopted but has had similar opportunities.

Noah agrees with Dan that he has never felt that he was rescued or saved. "I think things would have turned out a lot differently, but, really, how can I speculate about how things would have turned out? I'm very happy with what happened to my life. That's all that matters. And I definitely think the fact that Danny and I are adopted has affected my relationship with Oogy. We all arrived here through circumstance. Maybe it's fate. Danny and I weren't born here. You didn't even know we existed till Golden Cradle called you. Well, that's what happened with Oogy. We didn't know he existed, but he was alive before he ever became part of our family. What would have happened to us if you had not adopted us? I mean, me and Danny and Oogy. We all come from some place else and now we're here and who knows how that happened?" Noah grinned. "Oogy's my brother," he said.

When he told me this, Noah knew nothing of my belief in the role fate had played in bringing Oogy to us. This is but one of the common elements that tie the boys and Oogy together. There are remarkable similarities in their stories. Perhaps this is why Oogy's integration into our lives has been seamless and complete.

The magnificent and wholly unanticipated rewards that have come our way from Oogy make it difficult for me to believe that anyone could have made a different decision than we did. On many occasions, I have somewhat glibly told people that I did not rescue Oogy, the police did. I simply brought him home. The truth is, I tell them, that Oogy rescued me.

Finally, I started to think about the implications of that statement.

Even though I was not conscious of it—and in fact, mirroring what my parents had taught me, pushed it down to the bottom of my being so that it seemed as if it had never happened—my sister's death and my parents' reaction to it understandably, inevitably, and irrevocably reverberated down the passage of the rest of my life.

Perhaps as a child, unable to understand the dynamics involved, I wished I had died instead of my sister so as to spare my parents their grief. I know that until I became a father and saw the value of life, I used to think that the moments in which I could feel most alive and could most appreciate the experience of being alive were in the proximity of danger and death. No doubt as a result, I spent several years with the U.S.D.A. Forest Service on an interregional Hotshot crew fighting forest fires. Hotshot crews perform the initial attack on large fires, flying and busing from one to another for weeks at a time. My friends on the crew and I treated it as a unique experience, full of laughs, but really we were willfully ignorant of the dangers we encountered on a regular basis. That did not mean, of course, that they were not there. We simply disregarded them: falling timber, crashing limbs, hurtling boulders, poisonous snakes, tons of slurry dropped from planes that could crush you and explode the fire around you, helicopters that could fall from the sky at any moment, fire waiting just on the other side of everything we did.

But I think that all of this may also explain my immediate attraction to Oogy. I saw *myself* in him. I saw the burning of the metaphoric fire that almost consumed him resonate in the way that fire had made me feel alive. I saw how death had had its way with both of us. Proximity to death had shaped us. For me, raising the boys had carried an element of self-doubt, which is why I have always told people that I think the boys turned out as well as they did despite me, not because of me. But with Oogy, with this dog, there was never a moment's doubt that all the returns would be positive. And I raised him as I tried to raise the boys, as I wish I had been raised: a full-contact relationship free of ambiguity as to their central place of importance to the family.

And Oogy had come back from the dead to be with me. Neither my sister nor my parents had been able to accomplish that. I could keep him alive. I knew how to make him happy. I had been unable to do that before. I could not keep my sister alive or bring joy and a sense of fulfillment to my parents.

But I could do it for Oogy.

The Journey Boats

We wanted to get the boys something unique for high school graduation gifts and were lucky enough to find hand-carved sculptures that the artist calls Journey Boats. The Journey Boats are symbols intended to represent exploration and passage.

The boats themselves are the long, flat-bottomed type the pharaohs used for hunting the marshes, an experience they considered to be sacred in nature. On the prow of each boat, a protective eye guides.

Based on photographs we supplied to the artist, she carved likenesses of both boys and Oogy in each of the boats. In Noah's boat, he wears a red shirt; Dan, wearing a blue shirt, sits behind him with his right hand on Noah's shoulder. These positions are reversed in Dan's boat. They are looking confidently ahead, ready for whatever it is they are going to encounter. They have always covered each other's back, so their positioning and the supportive hands on each other's shoulder represents that. While they are about to embark on separate explorations, their steadfastness and physical contact have an additional meaning: We know that because of the special bonds they have with each other, they will make the journeys loving and supporting each other along the way.

While the boats have similarities, as do the boys' lives, there are also differences that distinguish them from each other. The boats are different colors. The prow of one is adorned with a dove, which is both the bird that Noah let out of the Ark to find land and a symbol of peace, representing our hope that there will be peace for the boys throughout their respective journeys. On the prow of the other is a bee, the symbol of hard work and achievement; they have both been long aware of the necessary connection between the two.

An observation by Graham Greene is carved on the bottom of each boat: "There is always one moment in childhood when the door opens and lets the future in."

Oogy has been and always will be an important and integral part of their lives, and thus their journeys, and they have always been appreciative of the unique and exceptional experience of having him in their lives. The love they have shared has not only been its own reward, Oogy's love for the boys has always been as meaningful to them as their love for him has been important to him. As a result, Oogy sits in each boy's boat; he will be with them forever. He sits in front of them, his right ear alert, staring ahead just as they do because, without fear, he is watching out for them, just as he always has and just as he always will.

Behind him, the boys are also watching over him. Just as they always have. Just as they always will.

Jennifer and I made a conscious decision not to include

ourselves in the boats. The boats are intended to symbolize the boys' explorations that are starting now that they have graduated high school. Everything that has happened before has simply led them to this point. Jennifer and I have brought them here and pushed them into the current that will take them into the rest of their lives. When Noah and Dan turn around, they will see us standing on the shore, growing smaller and smaller, waving and waving good-bye.

The only night in the last six and a half years that Oogy did not sleep with the boys was the night before each left for college. Dan left a week before Noah, and the night before Dan left, Oogy slept alone in Dan's room, on the clothes Dan had laid out on his bed to be packed in the morning for school. The same thing happened the night before Noah left: Oogy slept alone in Noah's room on the clothes he was going to pack for college.

He knew, somehow, that something out of the ordinary was occurring. At first I thought that he was trying to absorb the boys' scents so that he would have something to remember them by. Then it occurred to me that maybe Oogy might instead be leaving his scent to tell other dogs that the humans wearing these clothes were his. That they were already spoken for. He was imprinting their clothing as he had imprinted himself upon our lives.

During one visit to the first park Oogy and I frequented, we emerged from the trees into the parking lot by the creek to see two young men seated on the flatbed of a truck from which a small bulldozer had been off-loaded to clean up the busted glass, old tires, pieces of masonry, and other debris strewn about. They were wearing jeans, work boots, and orange T-shirts of the company they worked for. The one in charge was built like a fireplug. He had the sleeves of his T-shirt cut off; his arms were fully covered with multi-colored tattoos. A black bandana held back his long, dark hair and he sported thick hoop earrings a thick layer of stubble on his jaw. In another time he could have been a pirate.

He said, "Hello, pup. What's your name?" I told him and, as there was no threat, unclipped the leash so that Oogy could wander. The tattooed man asked what had happened, and when I told him the story, which included what Oogy had been bred for, he remarked, "Oh, he's Dogo."

I told him that he was one of fewer than a half-dozen people I had met who had recognized the breed. We talked a few minutes longer, and then I told him Oogy and I had to leave, as I needed to get home to start dinner and to help with homework. At that, the man jumped off the flatbed where he had been sitting and walked over to Oogy. He went down on his knees and took Oogy's face in his hands. He ran his hands over Oogy's face and smoothed back his ear. He rubbed his right thumb over the scar.

Then he nodded slowly, looked into Oogy's eyes, and said, "You made it, dude."

And he had.